200 Mexic

hamlyn | all colour cookbook

200 Mexican dishes

Emma Lewis

An Hachette UK Company
www.hachette.co.uk

First published in Great Britain in 2014 by Hamlyn
a division of Octopus Publishing Group Ltd
Endeavour House, 189 Shaftesbury Avenue
London WC2H 8JY
www.octopusbooks.co.uk

ISBN: 978-0-60062-824-8

A CIP catalogue record for this book is available from the
British Library

Printed and bound in China

10 9 8 7 6 5 4 3 2 1

Both metric and imperial measurements have
been given in all recipes. Use one set of measurements
only, and not a mixture of both.

Standard level spoon measurements are used in all recipes
1 tablespoon = 15 ml spoon
1 teaspoon = 5 ml spoon

Ovens should be preheated to the specified temperature –
if using a fan-assisted oven, follow the manufacturer's
instructions for adjusting the time and temperature.

Fresh herbs should be used unless otherwise stated.
Medium eggs should be used unless otherwise stated.

It is prudent for vulnerable people such as pregnant or
nursing mothers, invalids, the elderly, babies and young
children to avoid uncooked or lightly cooked dishes made
with eggs. Once prepared, these dishes should be kept
refrigerated and used promptly.

This book includes dishes made with nuts and nut
derivatives. It is advisable for people with known allergic
reactions to nuts and nut derivatives, or those who may be
potentially vulnerable to these allergies, to avoid dishes made
with these. It is prudent to check the labels of pre-prepared
ingredients for the possible inclusion of nut derivatives.

contents

introduction

introduction

You'll find food for every occasion in Mexico: quick and tasty street food, designed to be eaten on the go; complex and rich stews based on recipes that can be traced back to before the Spanish conquest of Mexico in the early 16th century; casual meals that have created a whole new Tex-Mex cuisine; and plenty of luscious puddings to round off a dinner with family or friends. With its hot and sunny climate, a whole wealth of foods that grow in Mexico have spread all over the world – who can imagine Italian food without the tomato or Indian food without the chilli?

Taking as its inspiration the fresh, vivid and gutsy flavours of Mexican cooking, this book will give you ideas for authentic moles and tamales as well as more modern-style food, such as nachos, salads and chilli con carne.

eating the mexican way

Breakfast is often a simple meal in Mexico, and then people might grab a quick bite later in the morning, perhaps from a street stall selling delicious tacos – soft tortillas with a variety of fillings and often topped with a salsa, or maybe a tamale, served in a steamed corn husk. Lunch is often eaten late, between 2 and 3pm. This is the main meal of the day and might start with some snacks – a guacamole perhaps – followed by one of Mexico's famous soups, then some simple grilled meat or fish, or alternatively, a complex stew with different nuts, spices and herb flavourings, and finishing with a sweet dessert.

the mexican larder

You can find everything you need to make Mexican food at home in larger supermarkets, but specialist grocers and on-line suppliers are a great source of more unusual ingredients.

chillies

Although chillies might provide the heat for many Asian curries, it's in Mexico that they have their origin and there is an astonishing variety on offer. Available fresh or dried in the hot sun, chillies are made into sauces and pastes with a variety of other flavourings, and these form the basis of many Mexican dishes. Different chillies have varying levels of heat and most of the heat is concentrated in the stem, seeds and membrane of the chillies, so remove these if you prefer a more mellow flavour.

One of the most popular types of chilli in Mexico is the jalapeño, which can be found fresh in many shops. Pickled jalapeños from a jar are also available and are used as a topping for nachos, and the chipotle – a dried and smoked jalapeño – has also become widely available. Look out for habañero or Scotch bonnet chillies, which are very hot, and dried ancho chillies, which have a citrusy taste and are perfect with fish and seafood. Anchos are dried poblano chillies. Sometimes also called pasilla chilli, this mild and tasty variety

is very popular in Mexico but can be hard to find fresh elsewhere. If you are lucky enough to get hold of some, try roasting a batch and freezing for later use in salsas or salads.

Chilli peppers owe their pungent heat to a chemical compound called capsaicin – the more capsaicin, the more fiery the chilli. The Scoville scale indicates the 'heat rating' of different types of peppers:

Bell pepper	0
Anaheim/New Mexico	500–1,000
Ancho	1,000–1,500
Mulato	1,000–1,500
Pasilla/Poblano	1,000–1,500
Guajillo	2,500–5,000
Jalapeño	2,500–5,000
Serrano	10,000–23,000
Arbol	15,000–30,000
Chipotle	15,000–30,000
Morita	15,000–30,000
Cayenne (Tabasco)	30,000–50,000
Piquin	50,000–100,000
Habañero	100,000–350,000

beans

Mexicans love their beans; big pots of legumes are simmered with some aromatics, while leftovers are often turned into tasty refried beans. A massive variety of beans are available both in Mexico and the UK, some of which are very attractive and will brighten up an easy summery salad dish. Look out for velvety black beans, borlotti and the red-streaked cranberry beans.

corn

Corn is so important to Mexicans that in Aztec times it was offered as a sacrifice to the gods. It is found everywhere in Mexico – most commonly, vivid yellow corn, but white types and a dramatic-looking blue corn are also available. It has many uses in cooking from an addition to milky drinks, such as atole, to grilled cobs of corn and even popcorn. It is also dried and ground with lime to make masa, the dough which is the base of tortillas. If you're lucky enough to live near a Mexican market, you might find this fresh, but most often it is dried and sold as masa harina (in the south of the country, the staple tortilla is made from corn while in the north they may be made from wheat).

The corn husks are also used and after drying out, they can be wrapped around fillings and steamed to make tamales. You might also come across huitlacoche, a fungus that grows on corn and is prized for its earthy flavour tempered with a little sweetness from the corn.

avocado

Hass avocados, with their bumpy dark skin and creamy flesh, are the most popular variety in Mexico. Always check whether an avocado is ripe: the flesh should be firm, but yield a little when gently pressed. If it is not quite ready yet, leave the avocado in a sunny place, and preferably next to some bananas, to ripen up. Try to avoid using hard and unripe avocados as the taste is just not the same.

Mexicans also use avocado leaves in their cooking. These are hard to get hold of but if you do find some, you wil find they have an aromatic taste a little like star anise and are especially good simmered in a pot of beans.

tomatillo

These are related to the cape gooseberry and taste tart and citrusy. They add a lovely fresh flavour to salsas and it's worthwhile seeking out specialist suppliers to get hold of some. Tomatillos are also available canned, or you could always use green tomatoes as a substitute instead.

cheeses

Cheese only began to be made in Mexico post-conquest with the introduction of milk, but it is now much loved, adding a tang to tacos and salads or richness to quesadillas. It's very hard to find authentic Mexican cheese outside of the country, but there are lots of good alternatives you can use instead.

Soured cream or crème fraîche is similar to Crema Mexicana, which is excellent for drizzling over dishes. Queso fresco is salty and has a crumbly texture, so feta cheese is

a good alternative, while mozzarella is similar to the string cheeses used in some Mexican recipes and melts very well.

herbs

Coriander is often used in Mexican cooking, and the fresh flavour brightens up many types of salsa. The leaves of this herb are great for garnishing a dish, but you can also use the coriander roots, which have lots of flavour, in cooking. Mexicans also use a type of oregano that has a more punchy taste than the Mediterranean varieties commonly found in Europe, as well as hints of citrus and liquorice.

A strong aromatic herb called epazote is also used in Mexican cooking. It grows wild in Mexico, Central America and parts of the United States but is available by mail order elsewhere. With a pungent taste a little like anise or tarragon, it is most commonly used to flavour stewed beans. To keep your herbs fresh, wrap them in a piece of wet kitchen towel before placing them in the fridge.

spices

Allspice berries are traditionally cultivated in Mexico although they are now used all over the world. An essential spice in Mexican

food, the small dark berries look a little like peppercorns and are good for grinding up and adding to many kinds of moles and stews. Cumin seeds and coriander seeds are also popular for adding extra flavour to a wide variety of dishes. Keep an eye out for Mexican cinnamon, too. It's found in lots of recipes, and the softer sticks are a little sweeter and mellower than other varieties of cinnamon.

vanilla

These densely flavoured pods are originally from Mexico and are great to use in puddings. Vanilla is especially good when teamed up with dairy products. The dried pods are full of seeds and when using them, you'll need to split the pods open carefully with a small, sharp knife and then scrape out the seeds. You can add the pod to a jar of sugar to make a lightly flavoured vanilla sugar, perfect for baking. Vanilla pods are expensive to buy, but you can also find pastes where the hard work of scraping away the seeds has been done for you. Good-quality extracts are also worth spending a little money on, but vanilla essence, which often tastes tart and synthetic, is best avoided.

chocolate

Chocolate is perhaps the best-loved ingredient Mexico has given to the rest of the world. Traditionally, however, chocolate wasn't sweetened but was used in rich mole sauces for savoury dishes. You'll find that a little dark

chocolate added to chilli con carne or other stews will give an extra earthy, rich flavour to the dish. Mexicans now also enjoy it as a sweet treat, often flavouring it with spices such as cinnamon, cloves and even chilli.

tequila

Few can resist a tequila – straight or mixed into a cocktail – to drink with a Mexican feast. Look out for authentic tequila, which should be made from 100 per cent agave plant – tequila from the blue agave is the best. Tequila is divided into three types: blanco tequila is young tequila; reposado has been aged for 2–12 months and is mellower; añejo is between 1 and 3 years old and so smooth it can be sipped like cognac.

equipment

You don't need a kitchen full of specialist equipment to cook Mexican food, but you may want to invest in one or two key items if you enjoy making corn tortillas from scratch, for example (see recipe on page 160).

tortilla press

These metal presses take the hard work out of making tortillas – the two discs press down on a small piece of dough to make a thin circle, perfect for cooking. You can use a chapatti press in a similar fashion.

griddle pan

A flat, heavy griddle or cast iron frying pan is useful for Mexican cooking and is known as a comal. These are perfect for making tortillas with lightly charred edges or for dry-roasting raw vegetables to make a salsa.

molcajete

Mexican-style pestle and mortars have been used for thousands of years for grinding ingredients. These distinctive pots, often carved from a single piece of basalt, have three legs to stand on and are perfect for grinding spices or making rough salsas. They often have decorative carvings and are great to use as serving dishes at the table. As basalt is porous, the molcajete absorbs flavours and regular usage will make your finished dishes uniquely flavoured.

cooking techniques

While high temperatures and open flames bring out the best in many Mexican ingredients, some delicious dishes, from salsa and guacamole to ceviche, can be prepared without the need for a cooker – just make sure to use the very best fresh ingredients you can find.

dry-roasting foods

Mexican cooks love to add a smoky dimension to their food, which gives a real depth of flavour. They often do this by dry-frying or grilling flavourful ingredients – typically onions, garlic, chilli and tomatoes – rather than cooking them in oil. This technique goes against most of the European cooking principles you will be used to – the vegetables will burn and you need to keep cooking until they are soft. Charred edges are what you are looking for in order to capture the taste of Mexico.

difference in taste and it makes them much easier to roll up and eat. This can be done in a number of ways:

- Loosely wrap the tortillas in foil, then place in a medium oven for 3–5 minutes until soft
- Place them in a steamer (Asian bamboo ones are great for this) for a couple of minutes
- To add extra flavour, hold the tortilla over a flame using tongs until lightly charred and pliable.

ceviche

This increasingly popular way of preparing fish and seafood involves marinating the raw ingredients in the juice of a citrus fruit, most commonly lime. The proteins in the fish are changed by the citric acid, so after being left in the marinade for a little while the fish will look opaque and 'cooked'. Apart from being delicious, this is a really fresh and healthy way of preparing fish, but the marinating will not destroy any bacteria, unlike cooking with heat, so make sure you use only the freshest, best-quality fish for ceviche, just as you would when making sushi.

softening tortillas

It's important to soften pre-cooked tortillas before serving – you'll really notice a

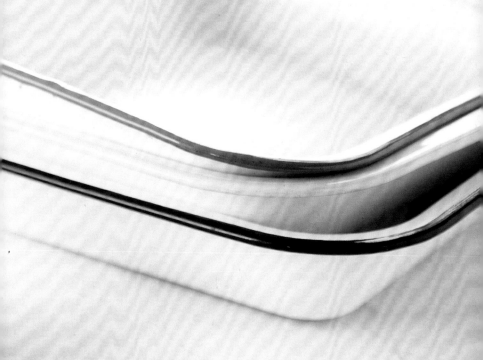

starters & snacks

guacamole

Serves **6**
Preparation time **10 minutes**

3 ripe **avocados**
1 **tomato**, finely chopped
handful of **coriander leaves**,
   finely chopped
½ teaspoon **ground cumin**
squeeze of **lime juice**
salt
tortilla chips, to serve

Halve and stone the avocados, then scoop the flesh out of the shells and place in a bowl.

Add the tomato, chopped coriander and cumin and roughly mash together with a fork. Stir in the lime juice and season to taste with salt.

Serve immediately with tortilla chips for dipping.

For watermelon guacamole, mash together the avocados with 150 g (5 oz) skinned, deseeded and chopped watermelon and ½ finely chopped green chilli (deseeded, if liked) in a bowl. Stir in the chopped coriander and some grated lime rind and season to taste with salt and lime juice. Serve as above.

mushroom quesadillas

Serves **4**
Preparation time **10 minutes**
Cooking time **15 minutes**

1 tablespoon **olive oil**
1 **shallot**, finely chopped
200 g (7 oz) **mixed mushrooms**
1 **garlic clove**, finely chopped
4 **wheat tortillas**
125 g (4 oz) **Cheddar cheese**, grated
salt and **pepper**
25 g (1 oz) **feta cheese**, crumbled, to serve

Salsa
100 g (3½ oz) **baby tomatoes**, chopped
squeeze of **lime juice**
handful of **coriander leaves**, chopped
salt, to taste

Heat the oil in a large frying pan, add the shallot and cook for 3 minutes until softened. Add the mushrooms and cook for a further 3 minutes until golden. Add the garlic and cook for 1 minute, then season.

Arrange the mushroom filling over half of each tortilla, sprinkle over the Cheddar and fold over.

Heat a frying pan until smoking hot. Place 1 quesadilla in the pan and cook for 1–2 minutes until lightly crisp. Carefully turn the quesadilla over and cook for a further 1–2 minutes until the cheese has melted. Remove from the pan and keep warm. Repeat with the remaining quesadillas.

Meanwhile, make the salsa by mixing together all the ingredients in a bowl.

Cut the quesadillas into wedges, then spoon over a little salsa and serve sprinkled with the feta.

For spicy mushroom bites, cut out 8 x 5 cm (2 inch) diameter rounds from 4 wheat tortillas. Brush over 2 teaspoons oil and place on a baking sheet. Cook in a preheated oven, 200°C (400°F), Gas Mark 6, for 3–5 minutes until crisp. Meanwhile, cook the mushroom mixture as above. Add ½ teaspoon of chipotle sauce with the garlic, then scatter over a handful of chopped coriander. Divide the mixture among the tortillas and spoon over a little soured cream to serve.

crispy cheese tubes

Serves **4**
Preparation time **10 minutes**
Cooking time **10 minutes**

8 corn tortillas
150 g (5 oz) **ricotta cheese**,
   drained
50 g (2 oz) **feta cheese**,
   crumbled
75 g (3 oz) **Cheddar cheese**,
   grated
2 tablespoons **vegetable oil**
salt and **pepper**

To serve
½ **Romaine lettuce**, shredded
4 **radishes**, sliced
1 **tomato**, chopped
juice of 1 **lime**

Wrap the tortillas loosely in foil and place on a baking sheet. Warm through in a preheated oven, 220°C (450°F), Gas Mark 8, for 3–5 minutes to soften.

Place the cheeses in a bowl and mix together, then season. Divide the mixture among the tortillas, spreading it down the centre of each one, then roll up tightly and place in a lightly greased baking tray, seam-side down. Brush over the oil and place in the oven for 5–10 minutes until golden and crisp.

Arrange the lettuce, radish and tomato on a serving dish. Squeeze over the lime juice to taste and season with a little salt. Top with the cheese tortillas and serve.

For cheese, potato & tomato bites, cook 1 large peeled and quartered potato in a saucepan of boiling water until soft, then drain well and return to the pan. Meanwhile, heat 1 tablespoon of vegetable or olive oil in a frying pan, add 1 finely chopped onion and fry for 5 minutes until softened. Add the onion to the potato with 125 g (4 oz) grated Cheddar cheese and 1 chopped tomato and mash together. Warm the tortillas in the oven as above, then spoon a little of the mixture along the centre of each one. Roll up and secure with cocktail sticks. Fill a large saucepan one-third full of vegetable oil and heat to 180–190°C (350–375°F), or until a cube of bread browns in 15 seconds. Deep-fry the filled tortillas in batches for about 5 minutes until golden and browned.

bean dip with coriander pesto

Serves **4–6**
Preparation time **10 minutes**,
  plus cooling
Cooking time **3 minutes**

400 g (13 oz) can **cannellini
  beans**, rinsed and drained
½ teaspoon **ground cumin**
2 tablespoons **water**
2 tablespoons **olive oil**
3 tablespoons **soured cream**
1 small **garlic clove**, crushed
salt and **pepper**
crispy **tortilla chips,** to serve
  (see page 160)

Pesto
25 g (1 oz) hulled **pumpkin
  seeds**
2 tablespoons **olive oil**
large handful of **coriander
  leaves**
grated rind and juice of ½ **lime**

Place the cannellini beans, cumin, measurement
water, oil, soured cream and garlic in a food processor
or blender and blend until smooth. Season to taste.
Transfer to a serving bowl and set aside.

Make the pesto. Heat a small, dry nonstick frying
pan, add the pumpkin seeds and dry-fry for 2 minutes
until very lightly toasted. Leave to cool, then chop the
seeds until small. Alternatively, whizz the seeds in a
mini food processor. Stir together the chopped seeds,
the oil, coriander, lime juice and rind in a bowl and
season to taste.

Swirl the pesto over the white bean dip and serve with
crispy tortilla chips.

For bean soup with coriander pesto, heat
1 tablespoon olive oil in a pan, add 1 chopped onion and
cook for 5 minutes until softened. Add 500 ml (17 fl oz)
vegetable stock, 150 ml (¼ pint) double cream and a
rinsed and drained 400 g (13 oz) can cannellini beans.
Bring to the boil, then reduce the heat and simmer for
10 minutes. Meanwhile, make the pesto as above. Whizz
the soup until puréed using a hand-held stick blender,
then ladle into bowls and swirl over the pesto to serve.

nachos with chipotle sauce

Serves **4**

Preparation time **15 minutes**, plus cooling

Cooking time **20 minutes**

200 g (7 oz) packet **tortilla chips**

200 g (7 oz) canned **refried beans**

200 g (7 oz) canned **black beans**, rinsed and drained

1 **pickled jalapeño chilli**, drained and sliced

150 g (5 oz) **Cheddar cheese**, grated

Chipotle sauce

1 **onion**

3 **tomatoes**

2 **garlic cloves**, peeled and left whole

1 teaspoon **chipotle paste**

salt and **pepper**

To serve

1 **avocado**, stoned, peeled and chopped

handful of **cherry tomatoes**, halved

handful of **coriander leaves**

4 tablespoons **soured cream**

Make the chipotle sauce. Heat a large, dry nonstick frying pan, add the onion and cook for 5 minutes, turning frequently. Add the tomatoes and cook for a further 5 minutes, then add the garlic and continue to cook for 3 minutes, or until the ingredients are softened and charred. Transfer to a food processor or blender and whizz to a coarse paste. Leave to cool, then add the chipotle paste and season to taste. Set aside.

Place a layer of tortilla chips in a heatproof serving dish. Mix together the refried and black beans in a bowl, then spoon some of the beans over the chips and scatter with a layer of the chilli and cheese. Repeat the layers, finishing with a heavy layer of the cheese.

Bake in a preheated oven, 200°C (400°F), Gas Mark 6, for 7 minutes, or until the cheese has melted.

Scatter over the avocado, tomato and coriander, drizzle with the chipotle sauce and soured cream and serve.

For hot chicken nachos, heat 1 tablespoon vegetable oil in a frying pan, add 1 finely chopped onion and cook for 5 minutes until softened. Add 2 crushed garlic cloves and cook for 30 seconds, then add a 400 g (13 oz) can chopped tomatoes, 5 drops of chipotle sauce, a pinch of salt and season with pepper. Bring to the boil, then reduce the heat and simmer for 10 minutes, adding more water if necessary. Shred 2 ready-cooked chicken breasts with a fork, then stir into the sauce and cook for a further 5 minutes. Layer the chicken mixture with the tortilla chips and cheese and bake as above. Drizzle over some soured cream and serve scattered with coriander leaves.

melting chorizo wedges

Serves **4**

Preparation time **10 minutes**

Cooking time **10 minutes**

1 ready-roasted **red pepper**, sliced

125 g (4 oz) thinly sliced **chorizo**

4 **wheat tortillas**

100 g (3½ oz) **Cheddar cheese**, grated

100 g (3½ oz) **mozzarella cheese**, thinly sliced

guacamole, to serve (see page 18)

Scatter the red pepper and chorizo over 2 tortillas, then sprinkle over the cheeses. Place the remaining 2 tortillas on top and gently press together.

Heat a dry nonstick frying pan until hot, add a tortilla and cook for 1–2 minutes until lightly browned, then carefully turn the tortilla over and cook for a further 2–3 minutes until the cheese has melted. Remove from the pan and keep warm. Repeat with the remaining tortilla.

Serve the tortillas cut into wedges with guacamole.

For seared chorizo with red pepper salsa, rub 1 tablespoon vegetable oil over 2 red peppers, then cook under a preheated hot grill for 10–15 minutes, turning frequently, until soft and charred all over. Place in a bowl, cover with clingfilm and leave until cool enough to handle. When cool, peel away the skin, remove the seeds and membrane, then finely chop the flesh and transfer to a bowl. Add 1 tablespoon each of lime juice and olive oil, a pinch of ground cumin and a handful of chopped coriander and mix together. Set aside. Heat a little olive oil in a frying pan, add 150 g (5 oz) thickly sliced chorizo sausage and fry until golden and just cooked through. Serve with the salsa.

spicy bacon clams

Serves **6**

Preparation time **15 minutes**

Cooking time **15 minutes**

4 **streaky bacon rashers**

1 tablespoon **olive oil**

5 tablespoons **water**

24 **live clams**, cleaned
(discard any that don't shut
when tapped)

Salsa

1 teaspoon finely chopped **red onion**

1 **dried chipotle chilli**, finely
chopped

½ ready-roasted **red pepper**,
finely chopped

1 tablespoon **olive oil**

handful of **coriander leaves**,
chopped

squeeze of **lime juice**

salt

Cook the bacon under a preheated hot grill for
7–10 minutes, turning once, until crisp. Leave to cool
slightly, then thinly slice. Keep warm.

Make the salsa by mixing together all the ingredients
in a bowl. Season to taste with salt.

Heat the oil and measurement water in a large
saucepan, add the clams, cover and cook over
a medium heat for 5 minutes until the clams have
opened. Discard any that remain closed.

Transfer the clams to a serving plate. Spoon a little
of the chilli salsa into each one, then top with a little
crispy bacon. Eat straight from the shells.

For spicy clam & bacon pasta, cook and slice the
bacon as above. Heat 2 tablespoons olive oil in a large
saucepan, add 2 sliced garlic cloves and cook for
30 seconds. Pour in 125 ml (4 fl oz) dry white wine and
cook for 5 minutes. Add a 400 g (13 oz) can chopped
tomatoes, a pinch of sugar and 3–5 drops of chipotle
sauce and simmer for 15 minutes, adding a little water if
necessary. Add the prepared clams, cover and cook for
5 minutes until the clams have opened. Discard any that
remain closed. Meanwhile, cook 300 g (10 oz) spaghetti
in a saucepan of boiling water according to the packet
instructions. Drain and add to the clam sauce. Stir in
4 tablespoons soured cream and coat the pasta well.
Serve with chopped coriander or parsley, if liked.

black bean salsa

Serves **4**
Preparation time **10 minutes**
Cooking time **2–4 minutes**

2 **wheat tortillas**
1 teaspoon **olive oil**

Salsa
2 tablespoons **olive oil**
400 g (13 oz) can **black beans**, rinsed and drained
125 g (4 oz) **cherry tomatoes**, halved
2 **spring onions**, sliced
1 **fresh jalapeño chilli**, deseeded, if liked, and finely chopped
grated rind and juice of ½ **lime**
handful of **coriander leaves**, chopped
salt and **pepper**

Make the salsa by mixing together all the ingredients in a bowl. Season well.

Brush the tortillas all over with the oil, then cut into triangles. Place on a baking sheet and cook under a preheated grill for 1–2 minutes on each side until just crisp.

Spoon the salsa into a serving bowl and serve with the tortilla chips on the side for dunking.

For black bean bites, heat 2 tablespoons olive oil in a frying pan, add 1 finely chopped shallot and cook for 3 minutes until softened. Add 1 crushed garlic clove and ½ teaspoon ground cumin and cook for 1 minute, then add a 400 g (13 oz) can black beans, including the liquid. Add a little water and cook for a couple of minutes, then roughly mash with a fork and season. Toast the tortillas as above and arrange on serving plates. Spoon a little of the bean mash on to each chip and scatter over 1 finely chopped red chilli (deseeded, if liked), some crumbled feta and a handful of chopped coriander. Serve with lime wedges to squeeze over.

chilli caramel popcorn

Serves **6**
Preparation time **1 minute**
Cooking time **15 minutes**

1 tablespoon **olive oil**
125 g (4 oz) **popcorn kernels**
75 g (3 oz) **caster sugar**
2 tablespoons **water**
15 g (1 tablespoon) **butter**
¼ teaspoon **bicarbonate of soda**
½ teaspoon **chilli powder**

Heat the oil in a large saucepan over a medium heat for 1 minute. Add the popcorn and cook until the kernels start to pop, then cover and cook for 5–7 minutes, shaking occasionally, until the kernels have stopped popping. Remove from the heat.

Meanwhile, place the sugar and measurement water in a medium saucepan and bring to the boil, then reduce the heat and simmer until the mixture turns golden brown. Remove from the heat and add the butter, bicarbonate of soda and chilli powder.

Pour the caramel over the popcorn and stir well to coat, then spread out on a baking sheet lined with nonstick baking paper. Place in a preheated oven, 150°C (300°F), Gas Mark 2, for 10 minutes until dried out. Allow to cool for a couple of minutes before serving.

For lime & cumin popcorn, prepare the popcorn kernels as above. Meanwhile, mix together 1 tablespoon melted butter, 1 teaspoon chilli flakes, 1 teaspoon ground cumin and the grated rind and juice of ½ lime in a large bowl. Add the cooked popcorn and toss well to coat, then place on a baking sheet lined with baking paper and cook as above.

ham & cheese empanadas

Makes **8**
Preparation time **15 minutes**
Cooking time **15–20 minutes**

2 tablespoons **mayonnaise**
150 g (5 oz) **Cheddar cheese**, grated
50 g (2 oz) **feta cheese**, crumbled
1 **green chilli**, deseeded, if liked, and chopped
125 g (4 oz) **smoked ham**, chopped
500 g (1 lb) pack **ready-made puff pastry**
beaten egg, to glaze

Mix together the mayonnaise, cheeses, chilli and ham in a bowl.

Roll out the pastry on a lightly floured work surface until about 3 mm (⅛ inch) thick. Cut out 8–10 circles, approximately 12 cm (6 inches) in diameter, using a small plate. Place a spoonful of the mixture into the centre of each circle. Brush around the edges with some of the beaten egg, then fold the pastry over and use your fingers or a fork to crimp together the edges. Brush over the tops with the remaining beaten egg.

Transfer the empanadas to a baking sheet and bake in a preheated oven, 200°C (400°F), Gas Mark 6, for 15–20 minutes until golden and crisp. Serve warm.

For Mexican ham & cheese sandwiches, split 4 soft white rolls in half. Butter the cut sides well, then cook under a preheated grill for 1–2 minutes until golden. Spread 1 tablespoon canned refried beans over each roll, then top each with 1 thick slice of smoked ham. Scatter over 75 g (3 oz) grated Cheddar cheese. Return to the grill and cook until the cheese has melted. Serve topped with 1–2 drained and thinly sliced pickled jalapeño chillies and 1 sliced tomato.

chicken bites with salsa

Serves **6–8**
Preparation time **25 minutes**
Cooking time **10–12 minutes**

300 g (10 oz) **masa harina** or
   fine cornmeal
½ teaspoon **salt**
300 ml (½ pint) **hot water**
6 tablespoons **vegetable oil**
1 ready-cooked **chicken
   breast**, shredded

Salsa
1 **green chilli**, deseeded, if
   liked, and chopped
1 **garlic clove**, chopped
3 canned **tomatillos** or 1 large
   tomato
2 **spring onions**, chopped
handful of **coriander leaves**,
   chopped

Place the masa harina or cornmeal in a bowl and add the salt. Add the measurement water and 2 tablespoons of the oil and mix together to form a dough. Divide the dough into 16 equal pieces and roll each into a ball, then roll out on a lightly floured work surface to 5 cm (2 inch) diameter rounds. Alternatively, flatten the dough pieces using a tortilla press (see page 160).

Heat a large, dry nonstick frying pan until hot, add the half the tortillas and cook for 1–2 minutes on each side until just golden and a little charred. Repeat with the remaining tortilllas.

Meanwhile, make the salsa. Place all the ingredients in a food processor or blender and whizz to form a coarse purée.

Heat 2 tablespoons of the oil in a frying pan, add half the tortillas and cook for about 2 minutes on each side until golden. Remove from the pan and set aside. Repeat with the remaining tortilllas, adding more oil if needed.

Arrange the crispy tortillas on a serving plate, scatter over the chicken and drizzle over the salsa. Serve immediately.

For chicken tostadas, cut out 8 rounds from 4 corn tortillas using a 7 cm (3 inch) cookie cutter. Heat 2 tablespoons olive oil in a pan and cook the tortillas in 2 batches for 1–2 minutes on each side until crisp. Mix together 1 shredded ready-cooked chicken breast, 3 sliced radishes, 2 spring onions, a good squeeze of lime juice and a handful of chopped coriander in a bowl. Serve the tostadas topped with the chicken mixture.

omelettes with tomato sauce

Serves **4**
Preparation time **10 minutes**
Cooking time **15 minutes**

2 tablespoons **olive oil**
6 **eggs**, beaten
salt and **pepper**
25 g (1 oz) **feta cheese**,
    crumbled, to serve

Sauce
1 **shallot**
3 ripe **tomatoes**
1 **fresh jalapeño chilli**,
    deseeded, if liked
1 **garlic clove**, peeled and left
    whole
1 tablespoon **olive oil**
pinch of **dried oregano**
splash of **red wine vinegar**

Make the sauce. Heat a large, dry nonstick frying pan until hot, add the shallot and cook for 2 minutes. Add the tomatoes and cook for a further 2 minutes, then add the chilli and continue to cook for 2–3 minutes until starting to char. Stir in the garlic and cook until all the vegetables are lightly charred. Leave to cool slightly, then remove the blackened skin from the tomatoes and chilli. Transfer the flesh to a food processor or blender with the shallot and garlic and whizz to a coarse purée.

Heat the oil in saucepan, add the vegetable purée, oregano, vinegar and a little water if necessary and simmer for 10 minutes until thickened. Season well.

Meanwhile, heat a little oil in a small nonstick frying pan, add one-quarter of the eggs, season and swirl around the pan, then cook for 1–2 minutes until just set. Fold the omelette in half, slide on to a plate and keep warm. Repeat with the remaining eggs.

Spoon a little of the sauce over each omelette and serve sprinkled with the feta.

For potato omelettes with tomato sauce, make the sauce as above. Meanwhile, cook 1 large peeled potato in boiling water for 12 minutes until just softened. Leave until cool enough to handle, then cut into slices. Heat 2 tablespoons olive oil in an ovenproof frying pan, add 1 sliced garlic clove and cook for 30 seconds. Add the potato slices. Beat together 6 eggs and season. Pour over the potato, reduce the heat to low and cook for 10 minutes, or until just set. Scatter over 25 g (1 oz) grated Cheddar cheese, then cook under a preheated grill until melted. Cut into wedges and serve with the sauce.

soups &
salads

black bean soup

Serves **4**
Preparation time **10 minutes**
Cooking time **20 minutes**

2 tablespoons **vegetable oil**
1 **onion**, finely chopped
125 g (4 oz) **chorizo
  sausage**, chopped
1 **garlic clove**, chopped
1 teaspoon **ground cumin**
2 teaspoons **tomato purée**
400 g (13 oz) can **black
  beans**, including the liquid
500 ml (17 fl oz) **chicken
  stock**
1 teaspoon **dried oregano**
chipotle sauce, to taste
salt and **pepper**

To serve
chopped **red chilli**, deseeded,
  if liked
lime wedges

Heat the oil in a large saucepan, add the onion and cook for 3 minutes. Add the chorizo and fry until golden. Stir in the garlic, cumin and tomato purée until well coated and cook for a further 1 minute.

Add the beans and liquid, stock, oregano and chipotle sauce to taste. Bring to the boil, then reduce the heat and simmer for 15 minutes. Season to taste.

Ladle the soup into serving bowls. Sprinkle over the chopped chilli and top with a lime wedge.

For black bean & chorizo salad, toss together a rinsed and drained 400 g (13 oz) can black beans, 2 chopped spring onions, 2 chopped tomatoes and 2 tablespoons olive oil and season well. Stir in 75 g (3 oz) sliced chorizo, a good squeeze of lime juice and some chopped coriander. Arrange on a serving plate and scatter over 50 g (2 oz) crumbled feta cheese and 1 finely chopped red chilli (deseeded, if liked).

avocado soup

Serves **4**

Preparation time **15 minutes**, plus cooling

Cooking time **15 minutes**

1 tablespoon **vegetable oil**

1 **onion**, finely chopped

1 **fresh jalapeño chilli**, deseeded, if liked, and chopped

1 **garlic clove**, chopped

900 ml (1½ pints) **chicken stock**

3 large **avocados**

juice of **1 lime**

salt and **pepper**

To serve

100 g (3½ oz) small cooked **peeled prawns**

handful of **coriander leaves**, chopped

4 crushed **ice cubes**

Heat the oil in a large saucepan, add the onion and cook for 5 minutes until softened. Add the chilli and garlic, then pour in the chicken stock and bring to the boil. Reduce the heat and simmer for 10 minutes. Whizz the stock until smooth using a hand-held stick blender, then leave to cool completely.

When ready to serve, stone and peel the avocados, then place in a food processor or blender with the cooled stock and whizz until smooth. Stir in the lime juice and season to taste.

Ladle the soup into bowls, then top with the prawns. Scatter with the coriander and sprinkle over some crushed ice to serve.

For hot avocado soup, heat 1 tablespoon olive oil in a saucepan, add the onion and cook for 5 minutes until softened. Add the chicken stock and 1 peeled and quartered potato and simmer for 15 minutes until the potato is soft. Pour in 150 ml (5 fl oz) double cream and heat through. Season well. Whizz the soup until smooth in a blender or using a hand-held stick blender. Whizz together 2 stoned and peeled avocados in a food processor or blender until smooth. Stir through the avocado purée. Serve scattered with chopped coriander leaves and 1 chopped tomato.

chicken & tortilla soup

Serves **6**
Preparation time **15 minutes**
Cooking time **25 minutes**

6 tablespoons **olive oil**
1 **onion**, chopped
2 **garlic cloves**, chopped
1 teaspoon **ground cumin**
50 g (2 oz) **polenta**
400 g (13 oz) can **chopped tomatoes**
1.5 litres (2½ pints) **vegetable stock**
5 drops of **chipotle sauce**
pinch of **sugar**
2 **corn tortillas**, thinly sliced
1 ready-cooked **chicken breast**, shredded
salt and **pepper**

To serve
1 **avocado**, stoned, peeled and diced
lime wedges
handful of **coriander leaves**, chopped

Heat 4 tablespoons of the oil in a large saucepan, add the onion and cook for 5 minutes until softened. Add the garlic, cumin and polenta and cook for a further 1 minute.

Stir in the tomatoes, stock, chipotle sauce and sugar and season. Bring to the boil, then reduce the heat and simmer for 15 minutes.

Meanwhile, heat the remaining oil in a frying pan, add the tortilla strips and cook for 1–2 minutes until crisp and golden. Remove with a slotted spoon and drain on kitchen paper.

Whizz the soup until smooth in a blender or using a hand-held stick blender. Stir half the chicken into the soup, then ladle the soup into bowls. Top with the remaining chicken, tortilla strips and avocado. To serve, squeeze over some juice from the wedges and scatter with coriander leaves.

For spicy chicken broth, poach 2 chicken breasts in 1.5 litres (2½ pints) chicken stock for 10–15 minutes until just cooked through. Remove and leave to cool slightly. When cool enough to handle, shred the meat, discarding any skin or bones. Ladle the broth into serving bowls and add the chicken. Scatter over 3 chopped tomatoes, 2 sliced spring onions, 1 sliced green chilli (deseeded, if liked) and a handful of chopped coriander. Squeeze over lime juice before serving.

butternut squash & chilli soup

Serves **4**
Preparation time **10 minutes**
Cooking time **35 minutes**

1 **butternut squash**, peeled,
  deseeded and cut into
  wedges
3 tablespoons **olive oil**
1 **onion**, finely chopped
1 **garlic clove**, finely chopped
2 **red chillies**, deseeded, if
  liked, and chopped
1 litre (1¾ pints) **vegetable
  stock**
125 ml (4 fl oz) **soured cream**
salt and **pepper**

Toss together the squash and half the oil, then season.
Place on a baking sheet and bake in a preheated oven,
200°C (400°F), Gas Mark 6, for 30 minutes, turning
once, until soft and golden brown.

Meanwhile, heat the remaining oil in a large saucepan,
add the onion and cook over a low heat for 7–10
minutes until soft. Add the garlic and half the chillies
and cook for a further 1 minute.

Pour in the stock and bring to the boil, then reduce the
heat and simmer for 5 minutes. Add the cooked squash
and simmer for a further 5 minutes.

Whizz the soup until smooth in a blender or using a
hand-held stick blender, then stir in 3 tablespoons of
the soured cream and season.

Ladle the soup into bowls. Spoon over the remaining
cream and top with the remaining chillies.

For spicy butternut & coconut soup, cook the squash
as above. Meanwhile, cook the onion as above, then
add ½ teaspoon ground cumin with the garlic and chilli.
Pour in 900 ml (1½ pints) vegetable stock and 200 ml
(7 fl oz) coconut milk and continue as above, omitting
the soured cream and adding a handful of coriander
leaves when blending the soup. Serve with extra
coconut milk swirled over.

mango & crab salad

Serves **4**
Preparation time **15 minutes**

1 large **mango**, peeled, stoned
and diced
150 g (5 oz) **radishes**, sliced
150 g (5 oz) **rocket leaves**
2 **spring onions**, chopped
300 g (10 oz) **fresh white
crab meat**
handful of **coriander leaves**,
chopped
handful of **mint leaves**,
chopped

Dressing
juice of **1 orange**
grated rind and juice of 1 **lime**
1 **red chilli**, deseeded, if liked,
and chopped
5 tablespoons **olive oil**
salt and **pepper**

Make the dressing by mixing together all the
ingredients in a bowl, then season well.

Arrange the mango, radishes and rocket on a serving
plate and toss with 1 tablespoon of the dressing.

Scatter over the spring onions, crab meat and
herbs. Drizzle over the remaining dressing and
serve immediately.

For mixed seafood salad, cook 125 g (4 oz) large raw
peeled prawns in a saucepan of simmering water for
3 minutes until they turn pink and are cooked through,
then remove from the pan with a slotted spoon and
leave to cool. Add 4 plump scallops to the pan and cook
for 2 minutes until just cooked, then drain and leave
to cool. Cut the scallops into slices. Make the salad as
above, replacing the crab with the cooked seafood.

mexican caesar salad

Serves **4**
Preparation time **10 minutes**
Cooking time **15–20 minutes**

½ small **baguette**, torn or cut
  into bite-sized pieces
3 tablespoons **olive oil**
1 teaspoon **ground cumin**
2 boneless, **skinless chicken
  breasts**, about 125 g (4 oz)
  each
1 **Romaine lettuce**, leaves
  separated and sliced into
  bite-sized pieces
salt and **pepper**
1 **red chilli**, deseeded, if liked,
  and finely chopped, to serve

Dressing
1 small **garlic clove**
50 g (2 oz) **Parmesan
  cheese**, grated
50 ml (2 fl oz) **soured cream**
3 tablespoons **mayonnaise**
lime juice, to taste

Place the bread and 1 tablespoon of the oil in a bowl and toss together. Transfer to a baking sheet and cook under a preheated hot grill, turning once, until golden and crisp. Set aside.

Mix together another tablespoon of the oil and the cumin and season well, then rub over the chicken breasts. Heat a griddle pan until smoking hot, add the chicken and cook for 12–15 minutes, turning frequently, until charred and just cooked through. Leave to cool slightly, then cut into slices.

Make the dressing. Place the garlic, Parmesan, soured cream and mayonnaise in a mini food processor or blender and whizz until smooth, then add lime juice and salt and pepper to taste.

Arrange the lettuce, croutons and chicken on serving plates. Drizzle over the dressing and sprinkle with the red chilli to serve.

For Mexican prawn & tortilla salad, toss together 250 g (8 oz) raw peeled prawns, 5 drops of chipotle sauce and 1 tablespoon olive oil, then cook the prawns on a smoking hot griddle pan for 3–5 minutes until they are pink, charred and just cooked through. Brush 2 tablespoons olive oil over 2 corn tortillas in a heatproof dish, then scatter over 1 tablespoon grated Parmesan cheese. Place in a preheated oven, 200°C (400°F), Gas Mark 6, for 5 minutes until just crisp. Leave to cool, then break into pieces. Make the dressing as above, then arrange the Romaine lettuce on serving plates, top with the prawns and toasted tortillas and drizzle over the dressing to serve.

crunchy veg salad

Serves **4**

Preparation time **10 minutes**, plus standing

½ **head of white cabbage**, thinly sliced

2 **carrots**, thinly sliced

75 g (3 oz) **radishes**, thinly sliced

2 **spring onions**, thinly sliced

1 bunch of **coriander**, chopped

Dressing

1 teaspoon **cumin seeds**

1 **red chilli**, deseeded, if liked, and finely chopped

grated rind and juice of 2 **limes**

2 tablespoons **olive oil**

salt and **pepper**

Make the dressing by mixing together all the ingredients in a bowl. Season well.

Place all the remaining ingredients in a serving bowl, then toss together with the dressing. Leave to stand for 5 minutes before serving.

For Mexican-style coleslaw, place ½ large shredded red cabbage and 2 roughly grated carrots in a serving bowl. To make the dressing, mix together a pinch of ground cumin, 5 drops of chipotle sauce, 5 tablespoons mayonnaise and the grated rind and juice of ½ lime in a bowl, then stir in 4 tablespoons soured cream. Toss together the vegetables and dressing, season and serve.

sweetcorn & black bean salad

Serves **4**

Preparation time **10 minutes**, plus cooling

Cooking time **5 minutes**

2 **corn on the cobs**, husks removed

grated rind and juice of 1 **lime**

½ **red chilli**, deseeded, if liked, and sliced

½ teaspoon **ground cumin**

5 tablespoons **olive oil**

400 g (13 oz) can **black beans**, rinsed and drained

125 g (4 oz) **cherry tomatoes**, halved

1 **spring onion**, sliced

2 **baby gem lettuces**, broken into leaves

50 g (2 oz) **feta cheese**, crumbled

handful of **coriander leaves**, chopped

salt and **pepper**

Cook the corn cobs in a large saucepan of salted boiling water for 5 minutes until just cooked through. Drain and cool under cold running water. Using a sharp knife, slice the kernels away from the cobs.

Mix together the lime rind and juice, chilli and cumin in a large bowl, then stir in the oil. Season well. Add the corn kernels, black beans, tomatoes and spring onions and gently toss together with the lettuce leaves. Scatter over the feta and coriander to serve.

For griddled sweetcorn, bean & tortilla salad, brush 1 teaspoon vegetable oil over the corn on the cobs and cook in a hot griddle pan for 3–5 minutes, turning frequently, until charred. Leave to cool slightly, then slice off the kernels. Stir together a rinsed and drained 400 g (13 oz) can black beans, 1 cored, deseeded and chopped red pepper, 3 tablespoons olive oil, 2 sliced spring onions and a good squeeze of lime juice in a salad bowl. Add the griddled corn kernels, 1 head of Romaine lettuce, broken into leaves, and a large handful of tortilla chips and toss together.

mexican prawn cocktail

Serves **4−6**

Preparation time **15 minutes**,
   plus marinating

125 ml (4 fl oz) **passata**

grated rind and juice of ½
   orange

grated rind and juice of **1 lime**

1 tablespoon **tequila** (optional)

5 drops of **Worcestershire
   sauce**

5 drops of **Tabasco sauce**

2 **spring onions**, sliced

1 **tomato**, chopped

½ small **cucumber**, chopped

300 g (10 oz) large cooked
   peeled prawns

1 **avocado**

2 **baby gem lettuces**, broken
   into slices

handful of **coriander leaves**

salt and **pepper**

saltine crackers or **tortilla
   chips**, to serve

Stir together the passata, the rind and juice of the orange and lime, the tequila, if using, and Worcestershire and Tabasco sauces in a non-metallic bowl and season to taste. Add the spring onions, tomato, cucumber and prawns and mix together. Cover with clingfilm and leave to marinate in the refrigerator for 30 minutes.

When ready to serve, stone, peel and slice the avocado, then place in serving bowls or plates with the lettuce. Spoon over the prawn mixture and scatter with coriander leaves. Serve with saltine crackers or tortilla chips.

For warm spicy prawn salad, mix together ½ teaspoon ground cumin, 1 teaspoon chipotle paste and 1 tablespoon vegetable oil in a bowl. Add 200 g (7 oz) raw peeled prawns and toss together. Cook under a preheated hot grill for 1−2 minutes on each side until they are pink and just cooked through. Arrange 2 chopped baby gem lettuces, 1 stoned, peeled and sliced avocado and a handful of halved baby plum tomatoes on a serving plate. Squeeze over a little lime juice, then spoon the warm prawns on top. Drizzle with some soured cream, scatter over chopped coriander and serve.

avocado & tomato salad

Serves **4**
Preparation time **10 minutes**,
    plus cooling
Cooking time **2 minutes**

1 tablespoon **olive oil**
1 **corn tortilla**
2 **ripe avocados**
handful of **mixed salad leaves**
125 g (4 oz) **cherry tomatoes**,
    halved

Dressing
grated rind and juice of ½ **lime**
handful of **coriander leaves**,
    chopped
1 teaspoon **chilli powder**
¼ teaspoon **ground cumin**
75 ml (3 fl oz) **olive oil**
salt and **pepper**

Brush the 1 tablespoon oil over the tortilla, then cut into thin strips about 5 cm (2 inches) long. Cook under a preheated hot grill for 1 minute on each side, or until crisp and lightly browned. Leave to cool.

Meanwhile, make the dressing by mixing together the lime rind and juice, coriander, chilli powder and ground cumin in a bowl. Slowly drizzle in the oil, stirring all the time. Season well.

When ready to serve, stone, peel and slice the avocados, then arrange on serving plates with the salad leaves and tomatoes. Drizzle over the dressing and serve scattered with the toasted tortilla slices.

For griddled avocado salad, rub the surface of 2 halved and stoned avocados with 1 teaspoon olive oil and scatter with a pinch of ground cumin and plenty of salt. Cook cut-side down in a hot griddle pan for 3–5 minutes until lightly charred and soft. Peel away the skin and slice. Serve with 4 sliced tomatoes and a handful of green leaves. Squeeze over plenty of lime juice to serve.

coconut sea bass ceviche

Serves **4**

Preparation time **10 minutes**,
plus marinating

250 g (8 oz) very fresh
skinless sea bass, cut into
bite-sized pieces

juice of 5 **limes**

5 tablespoons **coconut milk**

1 tablespoon **olive oil**

150 g (5 oz) **cherry tomatoes**,
halved

1 **green chilli**, deseeded, if
liked, and chopped

large handful of **coriander
leaves**, chopped

coconut curls, toasted (these
can be bought ready-made)

salt and **pepper**

Place the sea bass in a glass bowl. Mix together the
lime juice and the coconut milk in a jug. Pour over the
fish, then cover with clingfilm and leave to marinate in
the refrigerator for 3 hours until the fish turns opaque
and white.

Drain the fish, reserving the liquid. Toss together
the fish, oil, tomatoes and chilli in a serving bowl. Stir
through 2 tablespoons of the reserved fish liquid,
then scatter over the coriander and coconut curls.
Serve immediately.

For scallop & mango ceviche, slice each of 12 plump
scallops into about 3–4 thick slices and place in a glass
bowl. Squeeze over the juice of 5 limes and leave to
marinate as above. Drain the scallops, reserving the
liquid. Stir together the scallops, 1 peeled, stoned and
diced mango, 1 sliced spring onion, 1 chopped red chilli
(deseeded, if liked) and a couple of tablespoons of the
liquid in a serving bowl. Serve scattered with chopped
coriander leaves.

squash & pumpkin seed salad

Serves **4–6**
Preparation time **10 minutes**,
  plus cooling
Cooking time **15–20 minutes**

1 tablespoon **olive oil**
1 small **butternut squash**,
  peeled, deseeded and sliced
200 g (7 oz) **baby spinach**
  leaves
50 g (2 oz) **feta cheese**,
  crumbled
25 g (1 oz) **pumpkin seeds**

Dressing
large handful of **coriander**
  leaves
1 **green chilli**, deseeded, if
  liked, and finely chopped
grated rind and juice of **1 lime**
5 tablespoons **olive oil**
salt and **pepper**

Rub the 1 tablespoon oil over the squash slices. Heat a griddle pan until smoking hot, add the squash slices in batches and cook for 7–10 minutes, turning once, until lightly charred and just cooked through. Leave to cool.

Make the dressing by mixing together the coriander, chilli, lime rind and a little of the lime juice in a bowl. Stir in the oil, then add more lime juice if needed and season well.

Arrange the spinach leaves and cooled squash on a serving plate. Drizzle over the dressing, then scatter with the feta and pumpkin seeds and serve.

For squash & chorizo salad, cook the squash as above. Cook 125 g (4 oz) chorizo sausage, sliced into thick strips, in the griddle pan for 1–2 minutes on each side until lightly browned. To make the dressing, mix together a good squeeze of lime juice and 2 tablespoons olive oil in a bowl, then stir in 4 tablespoons single cream. Add 1 chopped green chilli (deseeded, if liked) and a handful of chopped coriander leaves and season. Arrange the chorizo, squash and a 200 g (7 oz) bag mixed salad leaves on a serving plate and drizzle over the dressing.

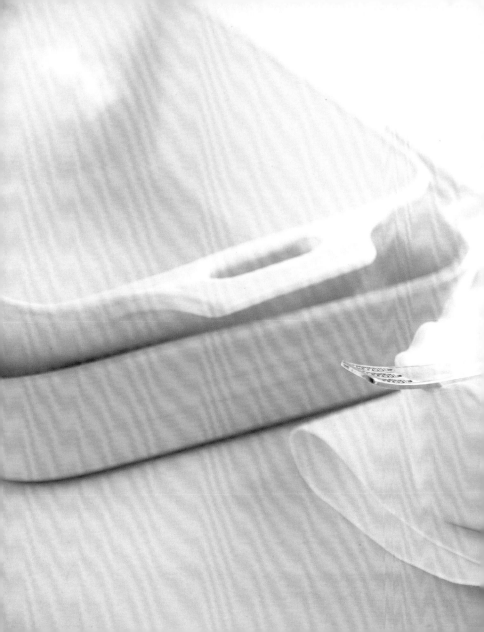

family meals

chilli pork ribs

Serves **2–4**

Preparation time **10 minutes**,
  plus marinating

Cooking time
  1 hour 40 minutes

1 small **onion**

2 **garlic cloves**, crushed

1 tablespoon **chipotle paste**

1 tablespoon **tamarind**

2 teaspoons **tomato purée**

1 teaspoon **dried oregano**

¼ teaspoon **ground
  cinnamon**

2 tablespoons **olive oil**

1 **rack of pork ribs**

salt and **pepper**

Place all the ingredients except the pork in a mini food processor or blender and whizz until smooth. Pierce the meat of the ribs a few times with a sharp knife, then place in a shallow dish. Rub over the marinade, cover with clingfilm and leave to marinate in the refrigerator for at least 4 hours and preferably overnight.

Remove about 3 tablespoons of the marinade and reserve. Wrap the ribs in a double layer of foil and place on a baking sheet. Bake in a preheated oven, 150°C (300°F), Gas Mark 2, for 1½ hours.

Remove the foil and baste all over the ribs with the reserved marinade. Heat a barbecue or griddle pan until smoking hot, add the ribs and cook for 3–5 minutes on each side until charred all over.

For braised beef short ribs, mix together 1 teaspoon each of ground coriander and ground cumin and rub over 8 beef short ribs in a shallow dish. Cover with clingfilm and leave to marinate in the refrigerator for at least 1 hour. Heat 2 tablespoons olive oil in a large frying pan, add the ribs, in batches if necessary, and cook for 5–10 minutes until browned all over. Remove from the pan and set aside. Add 1 finely chopped onion to the pan and cook for 5 minutes until softened. Stir in 2 crushed garlic cloves and cook for 30 seconds, then season. Add a 400 g (13 oz) can chopped tomatoes, 200 ml (7 fl oz) beef stock and 1 tablespoon chipotle sauce and bring to the boil, then return ribs to pan and simmer for 1½ hours until very tender. Squeeze over the juice of ½ lime, scatter with chopped coriander and serve.

chicken burgers & chipotle ketchup

Serves **4**

Preparation time **15 minutes**, plus cooling

Cooking time **45 minutes**

1 tablespoon **olive oil**

4 thin boneless, skinless **chicken breasts**, about 125 g (4 oz each)

4 **burger buns**

4 thin slices of **chorizo**

1 **avocado**, stoned, peeled and sliced

4 tablespoons **soured cream**

salt and **pepper**

Chipotle ketchup

1 tablespoon **olive oil**

1 **shallot**, finely chopped

2 **garlic cloves**, finely chopped

5 **tomatoes**, chopped

1 tablespoon **cider vinegar**

2 tablespoons **soft brown sugar**

2 teaspoons **chipotle paste**

To serve

potato chips dusted with **chilli powder**

Make the ketchup. Heat the oil in a small saucepan, add the shallot and cook for 5 minutes until softened. Add the garlic and cook for a further 30 seconds. Stir in the tomatoes and continue to cook for 3 minutes, crushing them with the back of a spoon. Add the vinegar, sugar and chipotle paste and simmer for 20 minutes until the liquid has evaporated. Season and leave to cool.

Rub the oil over the chicken and season well. Heat a griddle pan until smoking hot, add the chicken and cook for 10–15 minutes, turning once, until charred and cooked through. Remove from the pan and keep warm.

Place the buns, cut-side down, in the griddle pan and cook for 1 minute until toasted. Remove from the pan. Add the chorizo slices to the pan and cook for 30 seconds until starting to crisp.

Arrange the chicken breasts on the buns. Top with the chorizo, avocado slices, a spoonful of soured cream and a dollop of the chipotle ketchup.

Serve the burgers with potato chips dusted with a little chilli powder.

For Tex-Mex beef burgers, mix together ½ very finely chopped onion, 375 g (12 oz) minced beef, 50 g (2 oz) finely chopped chorizo sausage and a rinsed and drained 200 g (7 oz) can kidney beans in a bowl. Stir in 1 egg yolk and 1 teaspoon ground coriander and season well. Shape into 4 patties, then cook in a preheated griddle pan for 10 minutes, or until cooked to your liking, turning once. Serve on toasted buns as above, with sliced avocado, tomato salsa and soured cream.

turkey & pumpkin seed salad

Serves **4**
Preparation time **15 minutes**,
   plus cooling
Cooking time **5–6 minutes**

3 tablespoons **sunflower oil**
400 g (13 oz) **minced turkey**
1 ripe **avocado**
1 tablespoon sliced **pickled**
   jalapeño chillies
200 g (7 oz) can **sweetcorn**,
   drained
2 ripe **tomatoes**, chopped
1 small **red onion**, finely diced
small bunch of **coriander**,
   chopped

Dressing
juice of **2 limes**
1 teaspoon **clear honey**
4 tablespoons **pumpkin seed**
   oil
salt and **pepper**

To serve
½ small **red cabbage**,
   shredded
250 g (8 oz) **buffalo**
   mozzarella cheese, cubed
4 **taco shells**
3 tablespoons **pumpkin**
   seeds

Make the dressing by mixing together all the ingredients in a small bowl. Season to taste and set aside.

Heat the oil in a large frying pan and fry the turkey for 5–6 minutes until cooked and beginning to colour. Scrape into a bowl, mix with half the dressing and leave to cool.

Stone and peel the avocado, then cut into chunks and place in a separate bowl with the chillies, sweetcorn, tomatoes, red onion and coriander. Mix together, then add the remaining dressing and toss until combined.

Mix together the cooled turkey and sweetcorn salsa, then serve with the cabbage, mozzarella and taco shells, with the pumpkin seeds scattered over.

For turkey, white cabbage & sunflower seed salad, make the recipe as above, replacing the pumpkin seed oil with 4 tablespoons olive oil, the red cabbage with ½ small white cabbage, the mozzarella with 250 g (8 oz) finely diced Gruyère or Gouda and the pumpkin seeds with 3 tablespoons sunflower seeds. Omit the tacos, serving the salad as a base with the turkey mix on top.

baked spicy chicken legs

Serves **4**

Preparation time **10 minutes**,
plus marinating

Cooking time **45 minutes**

1 **onion**, chopped

4 **garlic cloves**, chopped

3 tablespoons **tomato purée**

1 teaspoon **ground cumin**

½ teaspoon **ground
cinnamon**

grated rind of 1 **orange**

1 tablespoon **red wine
vinegar**

1 tablespoon **soft brown
sugar**

1 **red chilli**, deseeded, if liked,
and chopped

handful of **coriander leaves**

4 tablespoons **olive oil**

8 **chicken legs**, about
100 g (3½ oz) each

salt and **pepper**

Place all the ingredients except the chicken in a food
processor or blender and whizz to a smooth paste.
Rub the paste all over the chicken, then place in a
non-metallic bowl and cover with clingfilm, or place in
a plastic food bag and seal. Leave to marinate in the
refrigerator for at least 3 hours and preferably overnight.

Tip the chicken on to a shallow baking tray and place
in a preheated oven, 200°C (400°F), Gas Mark 6, for
45 minutes or until the chicken is lightly charred and
cooked through, turning once. Serve with salads of
your choice.

For barbecued spicy chicken, marinate the chicken
as above, replacing the fresh coriander and chilli with
2 teaspoons chipotle paste. Heat a barbecue, then cook
the chicken for 20–25 minutes or until cooked through
and charred and crispy all over.

tamale pie

Serves **4**

Preparation time **20 minutes**

Cooking time **2 hours**

2 tablespoons **olive oil**

500 g (1 lb) **braising steak**, diced

1 **onion**, chopped

2 **garlic cloves**, crushed

1 **red chilli**, finely chopped

1 teaspoon **ground cumin**

½ teaspoon **ground coriander**

½ teaspoon **dried oregano**

2 teaspoons **cocoa powder**

400 g (13 oz) can **chopped tomatoes**

200 g (7 oz) can **kidney beans**, rinsed and drained

1 **red pepper**, cored, deseeded and chopped

salt and **pepper**

Topping

125 g (4 oz) **self-raising flour**

150 g (5 oz) **polenta**

1 **egg**, beaten

5 tablespoons **olive oil**

175 ml (6 fl oz) **milk**

50 g (2 oz) **Cheddar cheese**, grated

Heat 1 tablespoon of the oil in a large saucepan, add the beef, in batches if necessary, season and cook for 7–10 minutes until browned. Remove from the pan.

Add the remaining oil to the pan and cook the onion for 5 minutes until softened. Stir in the garlic, chilli, spices, oregano and cocoa powder and cook for 30 seconds, then add the tomatoes. Bring to the boil, then return the meat to the pan and simmer for 1 hour until tender, topping up with water if necessary.

Stir the beans and red pepper into the stew and cook for a further 15 minutes, then leave to cool slightly.

Meanwhile, make the topping. Tip the flour and polenta into a bowl. Whisk in the egg, oil and milk until smooth and season well with salt. Spoon the meat mixture into a medium-sized baking dish. Dollop over the topping, spaced slightly apart, then sprinkle with the cheese.

Bake in a preheated oven, 180°C (350°F), Gas Mark 4, for 35–40 minutes until golden and cooked through.

For turkey tamale pie, replace the beef with 500 g (1 lb) diced turkey and fry as above. Add a little more oil to the pan, add 1 finely chopped onion and cook for 5 minutes until softened. Stir in 1 crushed garlic clove, 1 teaspoon each of ground cumin and ground coriander and 1 teaspoon chipotle paste. Tip in the canned tomatoes, bring to the boil and simmer for 15 minutes. Add the red pepper and cook for 5 minutes, then stir through the browned turkey and spoon into a baking dish. Make the topping as above, adding a handful of chopped coriander leaves. Continue as above.

chilli con carne

Serves **4**

Preparation time **10 minutes**

Cooking time **45 minutes**

4 tablespoons **olive oil**

2 **red onions**, finely chopped

6 **garlic cloves**, finely chopped

500 g (1 lb) **lean minced beef**

1 teaspoon **ground cumin**

2 small **red peppers**, cored,
deseeded and diced

2 x 400 g (13 oz) cans
chopped tomatoes

2 tablespoons **tomato purée**

1 tablespoon **mild chilli
powder**

400 ml (14 fl oz) **beef stock**
(see right for homemade)

2 x 400 g (13 oz) cans **red
kidney beans**, rinsed and
drained

salt and **pepper**

Heat the oil in a saucepan, add the onion and garlic and cook for 5 minutes until softened. Add the mince and cumin and cook for a further 5–6 minutes, or until browned all over.

Stir in the red pepper, tomatoes, tomato purée, chilli powder and stock and bring to the boil, then reduce the heat and simmer gently for 30 minutes.

Add the beans and cook for a further 5 minutes. Season to taste and serve with brown rice.

For homemade beef stock, put 750 g (1 ½ lb) raw or cooked beef bones in a large, heavy-based saucepan with a large, unpeeled and halved onion, 2 carrots and 2 roughly chopped celery sticks, 1 teaspoon peppercorns and several bay leaves and thyme sprigs. Cover with cold water and heat until simmering. Reduce the heat to its lowest setting and cook very gently, uncovered, for 3–4 hours. Strain through a sieve and leave to cool. Store for up to 1 week in the refrigerator or freezer.

spicy pumpkin enchiladas

Serves **4**

Preparation time **15 minutes**

Cooking time **30–35 minutes**

400 g (13 oz) can
  **unsweetened pumpkin
  purée** (see below right for
  homemade)

75 g (3 oz) **feta cheese**,
  crumbled

handful of **coriander leaves**,
  chopped

8 **corn tortillas**

75 g (3 oz) **Cheddar cheese**,
  grated

salt and **pepper**

Sauce

1 tablespoon **olive oil**

1 **onion**, finely chopped

2 **garlic cloves**, finely chopped

1 teaspoon **ground cumin**

400 g (13 oz) can **chopped
  tomatoes**

1–2 teaspoons **chipotle paste**

Make the sauce. Heat the oil in a saucepan, add the onion and cook for 5 minutes until softened. Stir in the garlic and cumin and cook for 30 seconds. Add the tomatoes and chipotle paste and bring to the boil, then season. Reduce the heat and simmer for 15 minutes, topping up with water if needed.

Meanwhile, mix together the pumpkin purée, feta and coriander in a bowl, then season. Place a couple of teaspoons of the mixture on to each tortilla and roll up.

Spread about one-third of the tomato sauce over the base of a large baking dish. Place the tortillas in the baking dish, seam-side down. Spoon over the remaining sauce and scatter with the Cheddar.

Bake in a preheated oven, 200°C (425°F), Gas Mark 7, for 15–20 minutes until golden and bubbling.

For homemade pumpkin purée, cut 750 g (1 ½ lb) pumpkin or squash into large chunks, discarding any seeds. Toss together with 2 tablespoons olive oil and spread out on a baking sheet. Bake in a preheated oven, 180°C (350°F), Gas Mark 4, for 45 minutes, or until soft and lightly browned. Leave to cool slightly, then scrape away the flesh and whizz in a food processor or blender until smooth.

chargrilled chicken with salsa

Serves **4**

Preparation time **10 minutes**,
   plus marinating and resting

Cooking time **18 minutes**

2 tablespoons **dark soy sauce**
2 teaspoons **sesame oil**
1 tablespoon **olive oil**
2 teaspoons **clear honey**
pinch of **crushed dried
   chillies**
4 large boneless, skinless
   chicken breasts, about
   200 g (7 oz) each

Salsa
1 **red onion**, diced
1 small **garlic clove**, crushed
1 bunch of **coriander leaves**,
   roughly chopped
6 tablespoons **extra virgin
   olive oil**
grated rind and juice of
   1 lemon
1 teaspoon **ground cumin**
salt and **pepper**

Place the soy sauce, sesame oil, olive oil, honey and dried chillies in a shallow dish and mix together. Add the whole chicken breasts, cover with clingfilm and leave to marinate for 3–4 hours in the refrigerator.

Heat a griddle pan over a high heat until hot, add the chicken, reduce the heat to medium and cook for 8 minutes on each side until chargrilled and cooked through. Wrap in foil and leave to rest for 5 minutes.

Meanwhile, mix together all the salsa ingredients in a bowl, then season. Leave to infuse.

Strain the marinade juices into a small saucepan and bring to the boil, then remove from the heat.

Top the chicken with the salsa and the warm marinade and serve with couscous mixed with tomato.

For salmon with mango & chilli salsa, make
the marinade as above. Coat 4 salmon fillets, about 175 g (6 oz) each, in the marinade and leave at room temperature for 2 hours. Cook in a hot griddle pan for 2–3 minutes on each side until cooked through and slightly charred. Cut ½ peeled and stoned mango into small dice. Make the salsa as above, with only ½ diced red onion and omitting the garlic. Add the mango. Finely slice a bird's eye chilli (deseeded, if liked) and stir through the salsa. Serve the hot salmon with the salsa spooned over.

spicy seafood & bean stew

Serves **4**

Preparation time **15 minutes**, plus soaking

Cooking time **15 minutes**

1 **dried ancho chilli**, stem removed and deseeded

2 **garlic cloves**, peeled and left whole

½ teaspoon **dried oregano**

½ teaspoon **ground cumin**

5 **tomatoes**, chopped

2 tablespoons **olive oil**

200 ml (7 fl oz) **fish** or **vegetable stock**

400 g (13 oz) can **black beans**, rinsed and drained

300 g (10 oz) **live mussels**, scrubbed and debearded (discard any that don't shut when tapped)

325 g (11 oz) **sea bass fillet**, cut into bite-sized pieces

salt and **pepper**

To serve

cooked **white rice**

chopped **coriander leaves**

sliced **red onion**

lime wedges

Place the chilli in a small heatproof bowl, pour over boiling water and leave to soak for 20 minutes, turning occasionally, until softened. Drain well. Heat a large, dry, heavy-based frying pan, add the garlic and cook for 2 minutes on each side until browned and soft. Place the rehydrated chilli, garlic, oregano, cumin and tomatoes in a food processor or blender and whizz to a coarse sauce.

Heat the oil in the pan, add the tomato sauce and cook for about 5 minutes until reduced to a thick paste. Pour in the stock and bring to the boil. Add the beans and reduce to a simmer.

Add the mussels and fish and cook for 5–7 minutes until the fish is opaque and the mussels have opened. Discard any mussels that remain closed.

Spoon white rice into serving bowls and ladle over the stew. Sprinkle with coriander and red onion and serve with lime wedges.

For fish & sweetcorn soup, make the recipe as above, omitting the black beans and mussels. Use a sharp knife to slice away the kernels from 2 corn on the cobs and add to the soup with the fish and cook for 2 minutes. Stir in 250 g (8 oz) large raw peeled prawns and cook for a further 3 minutes until cooked through. Serve as above.

ranch eggs

Serves **4**
Preparation time **10 minutes**
Cooking time **25 minutes**

2 tablespoons **olive oil**
1 **onion**, sliced
2 **garlic cloves**, sliced
1–2 **red chillies**, deseeded, if
   liked, and chopped
2 x 400 g (13 oz) cans
   chopped tomatoes
pinch of **brown sugar**
3 **plum tomatoes**, thickly
   sliced
4 **eggs**
salt and **pepper**

To serve
75 g (3 oz) **Lancashire
   cheese**, crumbled
chopped **coriander leaves**
4 **wheat** or **corn tortillas**

Heat the oil in a large frying pan, add the onion and cook for 5 minutes until softened. Stir in the garlic and chillies and cook for a further 1 minute. Add the canned tomatoes and sugar and bring to the boil, then season. Reduce the heat and simmer for 10 minutes, topping up with water if necessary.

Add the plum tomatoes and cook for 3 minutes. Using the sliced tomatoes as a base, form 4 indentations in the sauce. Crack an egg into each one, cover with a lid or piece of foil and cook over a medium heat for about 5 minutes, or until the egg whites are cooked through.

Remove the lid and scatter over the crumbled cheese and chopped coriander, then warm through the tortillas in a preheated oven, 220°C (450°F), Gas Mark 8, for 3–5 minutes to soften.

Spoon some tomato and egg mixture into each tortilla and serve.

For fried eggs with smoky tomato sauce, make the tomato sauce as above, replacing the red chillies with 1–2 teaspoons chipotle paste. Replace the plum tomatoes with 1 cored, deseeded and chopped red pepper and cook for 5–10 minutes until soft. Heat 1 tablespoon olive oil in a large nonstick frying pan. Crack 4 eggs into the pan and cook for about 3 minutes until the whites are cooked through. Place the eggs on warmed tortillas and top with a little of the tomato sauce to serve.

chilli tacos

Serves **4**
Preparation time **10 minutes**
Cooking time **25 minutes**

2 tablespoons **olive oil**
1 **large onion**, finely chopped
2 **garlic cloves**, crushed
500 g (1 lb) **lean minced beef**
700 g (1 lb 7 oz) jar **passata**
400 g (13 oz) can **red kidney
    beans**, rinsed and drained
2–3 tablespoons **hot chilli
    sauce**
salt and **pepper**

To serve
8 soft **corn tortillas**
125 g (4 oz) **Cheddar
    cheese**, grated
125 g (4 oz) **soured cream**
handful of **coriander sprigs**

Heat the oil in a saucepan, add the onion and garlic and cook over a high heat for 5 minutes until softened. Add the minced beef and cook for 5 minutes until browned, breaking it up with a wooden spoon.

Stir in the passata, beans, chilli sauce and salt and pepper to taste and bring to the boil. Reduce the heat and simmer for 15 minutes until thickened.

Meanwhile, put the tortillas on a large baking sheet and warm through in a preheated oven, 220°C (450°F), Gas Mark 8, for 3–5 minutes to soften.

Place the tortillas on a serving plate in the centre of the table. Take 2 tortillas per person and spoon some chilli into each one. Top with a quarter of the cheese and soured cream and a little coriander, roll up and serve.

For lentil & red pepper chilli, fry the onion and garlic as above, adding 1 large cored, deseeded and chopped red pepper. Replace the beef with 2 rinsed and drained 400 g (13 oz) cans brown lentils and add with the passata, beans, chilli sauce and salt and pepper to taste. Bring to the boil, then reduce the heat and simmer for 15 minutes. Serve the chilli hot with cooked basmati rice, guacamole (see page 18) and soured cream.

pork & sweet potato bake

Serves **4**

Preparation time **15 minutes**

Cooking time **15–20 minutes**

2 tablespoons **olive oil**

1 teaspoon **ground coriander**

4 thick **pork chops**

4 **sweet potatoes**, peeled and
cut into wedges

4 **garlic cloves**, unpeeled

2 tablespoons **honey**

grated rind and juice of 1 **lime**

handful of **coriander leaves**,
chopped

1 **red chilli**, deseeded, if liked,
and sliced

2 **spring onions**, sliced

salt and **pepper**

lime wedges, to serve

Place the oil and ground coriander in a small bowl
and mix together, then season well. Toss the pork chops,
sweet potatoes and garlic in the oil and spread out on
a shallow baking tray. Place in a preheated oven,
220°C (425°F), Gas Mark 7, for 10 minutes.

Meanwhile, stir together the honey and lime rind
and juice in a bowl. Turn the meat and sweet potatoes
over, then drizzle over the honey sauce. Return to
the oven for a further 5–10 minutes until golden
and cooked through.

Scatter over the chopped coriander, chilli and spring
onions and serve with lime wedges.

For pork & sweet potato stew, heat 1 tablespoon
olive oil in a large saucepan, add 500 g (1 lb) cubed
pork and cook for 5–10 minutes until browned all over.
Remove from the pan and set aside. Add a little more
oil to the pan if needed and cook 1 chopped onion for
5 minutes until softened. Stir in 1 crushed garlic clove,
1 teaspoon each of ground cumin and ground coriander
and cook for 30 seconds. Pour in a 400 g (13 oz) can
chopped tomatoes and 1 tablespoon chipotle paste
and add a cinnamon stick. Return the pork to the pan
and simmer for 15 minutes, topping up with water.
Add 2 peeled and cubed sweet potatoes and cook for
a further 15 minutes until tender. Serve drizzled with
a little soured cream and chopped coriander leaves.

griddled chicken fajitas

Serves **4**
Preparation time **20 minutes**,
  plus marinating
Cooking time **20–25 minutes**

4 boneless, skinless **chicken
  breasts**, about 125 g (4 oz)
  each
4 large **flour tortillas**
1 **avocado**
150 ml (¼ pint) **soured cream**
4 **tomatoes**, skinned and
  sliced
4 **spring onions**, sliced
½ **red onion**, finely chopped
salt and **pepper**

Marinade
2 tablespoons **soy sauce**
3 cm (1¼ inch) piece of **fresh
  root ginger**, peeled and
  finely chopped
2 **garlic cloves**, finely chopped
2 tablespoons **olive oil**
1 bunch of **coriander**,
  chopped
1 **chilli**, deseeded, if liked,
  and chopped
2 tablespoons **lime juice**

Place all the marinade ingredients in a non-metallic bowl and mix well. Add the chicken breasts, cover with clingfilm and leave to marinate at room temperature for 2 hours or in the refrigerator for up to 24 hours.

Heat a griddle pan until hot, add the marinated chicken and cook for 8–10 minutes on each side until cooked through. Leave to cool slightly, then slice into long strips.

Warm the tortillas under a preheated grill for 30 seconds on each side. Stone, peel and slice the avocado. Spread a spoonful of soured cream over one side of each tortilla, then scatter over a little tomato, avocado and a sprinkling of spring onions and red onion.

Add the pieces of griddled chicken and season. Roll up each tortilla tightly and cut in half across each one. Serve with tortilla chips, if liked.

steak burritos

Serves **4**

Preparation time **25 minutes**, plus marinating

Cooking time **15 minutes**

2 **garlic cloves**, crushed

1 tablespoon **mild chilli powder**

1 tablespoon **olive oil**

2 teaspoons **smoked sweet paprika**

1 teaspoon **ground cumin**

400 g (14 oz) **skirt steak**

8 **wheat tortillas**

salt and **pepper**

Salsa

3 **tomatoes**, chopped

2 tablespoons finely chopped **red onion**

juice of ½ **lime**

Filling

200 g (7 oz) cooked **white rice**

150 g (5 oz) **black beans**, rinsed, drained and warmed through

sliced **iceberg lettuce**

grated **Cheddar cheese**

soured cream

chopped **coriander leaves**

Place the garlic, chilli powder, oil, paprika and cumin in a bowl and mix together. Rub all over the steak, then place in a shallow dish. Cover with clingfilm and leave to marinate in the refrigerator for at least 2 hours and preferably overnight.

Season the meat well. Heat a griddle pan until smoking hot, add the steak and cook for 3–5 minutes on each side until browned and cooked to your liking. Remove from the pan and cut into thin slices.

Make the salsa by tossing together all the ingredients in a bowl.

When ready to serve, heat a dry nonstick frying pan until hot, add 1 tortilla and cook for 30 seconds until pliable. Remove from the heat and spoon a little cooked rice and warmed beans into the centre. Add some strips of steak and top with some tomato salsa, lettuce, cheese, soured cream and coriander. Fold up the outside edges, squashing down the filling a little if necessary, and roll over so the filling is completely enclosed. Repeat with the remaining tortillas.

For chicken burritos, stir together 1 teaspoon ground cumin, handful chopped coriander, 2 tablespoons olive oil and rub over 4 skinless, boneless chicken thighs. Season well, then cook on a griddle pan for 7 minutes on each side until charred and cooked through. Prepare and roll up the burritos as above.

bean chilli with avocado salsa

Serves **4–6**
Preparation time **15 minutes**
Cooking time **30–35 minutes**

3 tablespoons **olive oil**
2 teaspoons **cumin seeds**,
  crushed
1 teaspoon **dried oregano**
1 **red onion**, chopped
1 **celery stick**, chopped
1 **medium-strength red chilli**,
  deseeded, if liked, and sliced
2 x 400 g (13 oz) cans
  chopped tomatoes
50 g (2 oz) **sun-dried
  tomatoes**, thinly sliced
2 teaspoons **sugar**
300 ml (½ pint) **vegetable
  stock**
2 x 400 g (13 oz) cans **kidney
  beans**, rinsed and drained
handful of **coriander leaves**,
  chopped
100 g (3½ oz) **soured cream**,
  to serve

Salsa

1 small **avocado**
2 **tomatoes**
2 tablespoons **sweet chilli
  sauce**
2 teaspoons **lime juice**

Heat the oil in a large saucepan, add the cumin seeds, oregano, onion, celery and chilli and cook gently for about 6–8 minutes, stirring, until the vegetables start to colour.

Add the canned tomatoes, sun-dried tomatoes, sugar, stock, beans and coriander and bring to the boil. Reduce the heat and simmer for about 20 minutes until the juices are thickened and pulpy.

Make the salsa. Stone, peel and finely dice the avocado, then place in a small bowl. Halve the tomatoes, scoop out the seeds and finely dice the flesh. Add to the bowl with the chilli sauce and lime juice. Mix well.

Season the bean mixture and spoon into bowls. Top with spoonfuls of soured cream and the avocado salsa. Serve with toasted pitta or flatbreads.

For bean stew, heat 4 tablespoons olive oil in a small saucepan, add 2 crushed garlic cloves, 1 tablespoon chopped rosemary and 2 teaspoons grated lemon rind and gently fry for 3 minutes. Add 2 x 400 g (13 oz) cans butter beans with their liquid, 4 large skinned and chopped tomatoes and a little chilli powder. Bring to the boil, then simmer over a high heat for 8–10 minutes until the sauce is thickened. Make the avocado salsa as above. Season the stew and serve with the avocado salsa and soured cream.

fish tacos with tartare sauce

Serves **4**
Preparation time **20 minutes**
Cooking time **10–15 minutes**

100 g (3½ oz) **plain flour**
2 teaspoons **ground cumin**
1 teaspoon **chilli powder**
2 teaspoons **dried oregano**
200 ml (7 fl oz) **cold water**
400 g (13 oz) **white fish**,
    skinned and sliced into thick
    strips
vegetable oil, for deep-frying
salt and **pepper**

Tartare sauce
100 g (3½ oz) **mayonnaise**
1 **fresh jalapeño chilli**,
    deseeded, if liked, and finely
    chopped
1 teaspoon **capers**, drained
1 small **gherkin**, finely
    chopped
grated rind and juice of ½ **lime**
handful of **coriander leaves**,
    chopped

To serve
¼ **red cabbage**, finely sliced
8 **corn tortillas**

Place the flour, spices, oregano and measurement water in a shallow dish and stir together until it resembles thick cream. Season the fish, then dip in the flour mixture until well coated.

Fill a large saucepan one-third full of oil and heat to 180–190°C (350–375°F), or until a cube of bread browns in 15 seconds. Let any excess drip away from the fish, then deep-fry in batches for 3–5 minutes until golden and crisp. Remove from the pan, drain on kitchen paper and keep warm.

Make the tartare sauce by mixing together the mayonnaise, chilli, capers and gherkin in a bowl. Add the lime rind and juice to taste, then stir in the coriander.

Toss the cabbage with a little salt and a dash of lime juice. Divide among the tortillas and add the deep-fried fish. Drizzle over the tartare sauce and serve.

For griddled fish tacos, mix together 3 tablespoons olive oil, 1 teaspoon sweet smoked paprika, ½ teaspoon each of ground cumin and ground coriander and a small handful of chopped coriander leaves in a bowl. Toss together with the fish pieces and season. Heat a griddle pan until smoking hot, add the fish and cook for 3–5 minutes on each side until charred and just cooked through. Serve on the tortillas as above.

crispy chicken bake

Serves **4**

Preparation time **15 minutes**, plus soaking

Cooking time **25 minutes**

vegetable oil, for deep-frying

6 **corn tortillas**, cut into triangles

3 **dried ancho chillies**, deseeded, if liked

6 large **tomatoes**

3 **garlic cloves**, peeled and left whole

250 g (8 oz) ready-cooked **chicken breast**, shredded

salt and **pepper**

handful of **coriander leaves**, chopped, to garnish

50 g (2 oz) **feta cheese**, crumbled, to serve

Fill a large saucepan one-third full of oil and heat to 180°C (350°F), or until a cube of bread browns in 15 seconds. Deep-fry the tortilla pieces in batches for about 30 seconds until golden and crisp. Remove with a slotted spoon and drain on kitchen paper.

Place the chillies in a heatproof bowl, pour over boiling water and leave to soak for 30 minutes.

Meanwhile, heat a dry nonstick frying pan until hot, add the tomatoes and cook for 10 minutes, turning frequently, until starting to char. Add the garlic and cook for a further 2 minutes until charred all over. Transfer to a food processor or blender.

Drain the chillies, reserving the water. Add to the blender with 2 tablespoons of the soaking water and whizz to a smooth paste. Transfer the paste to a saucepan, add the chicken, season and simmer for 5 minutes.

Place the deep-fried tortilla chips in a heatproof serving dish, then pour the sauce all over the chips. Place in a preheated oven, 160°C (325°F), Gas Mark 3, for 5 minutes, or until heated through. Scatter with the coriander and feta.

For quick crispy chicken bake, place 500 ml (17 fl oz) tomato pasta sauce and 1–2 teaspoons chipotle paste in a saucepan and simmer for 5 minutes. Stir in the shredded chicken and cook for a further 5 minutes. Tip 250 g (8 oz) natural corn chips into a serving dish. Pour over the chicken sauce and top with 50 g (2 oz) grated Cheddar cheese. Bake as above, then scatter the chopped coriander leaves to serve.

baked turkey burritos

Serves **4**
Preparation time **12 minutes**
Cooking time **30–35 minutes**

4 tablespoons **vegetable oil**
500 g (1 lb) **turkey breast**,
    thinly sliced
1 large **onion**, sliced
1 **red pepper**, cored,
    deseeded and sliced
1 **yellow pepper**, cored,
    deseeded and sliced
150 g (5 oz) can **red kidney
    beans**, rinsed and drained
150 g (5 oz) **cooked rice**
juice of **1 lime**
8 **flour tortillas**
6 tablespoons **medium-hot
    ready-made salsa**
2 tablespoons sliced **pickled
    jalapeño chillies** (optional)
250 g (8 oz) **Cheddar
    cheese**, grated
salt and **pepper**

To serve (optional)
guacamole (see page 18)
½ **iceberg lettuce**, shredded
Tomato & Chilli Salsa (see
    right)

Heat 2 tablespoons of the oil in a large frying pan, add the sliced turkey and fry for 3–4 minutes, stirring, until it is beginning to colour, then remove with a slotted spoon and set aside.

Increase the heat, add the remaining oil and fry the onion and peppers for 5–6 minutes, stirring occasionally, so that they colour quickly without softening too much. Reduce the heat, return the turkey to the pan and stir in the beans and cooked rice. Season well, add the lime juice and remove from the heat.

Spoon the filling on to the tortillas, roll them up and arrange in a rectangular ovenproof dish. Pour the salsa over the tortillas and scatter over the jalapeño chillies, if using, and cheese.

Bake in a preheated oven, 200°C (400°F), Gas Mark 6, for about 20 minutes, until hot and the cheese has melted. Serve immediately with guacamole, shredded lettuce and Tomato & Chilli Salsa, if liked.

For tomato & chilli salsa, to serve as an accompaniment, place 500 g (1 lb) chopped tomatoes, 1 chopped hot red chilli (deseeded, if liked), 1 chopped garlic clove, 1 chopped small onion, 2 tablespoons tomato purée, 2 tablespoons red wine vinegar and 2 tablespoons sugar in a bowl and mix well. Alternatively, blend all the ingredients in a food processor until finely chopped.

food for friends

chicken & chorizo enchiladas

Serves **4**
Preparation time **20 minutes**
Cooking time **40–45 minutes**

4 large bone-in **chicken breasts**, skin removed
125 g (4 oz) cooked **chorizo sausage**, diced
150 g (5 oz) **crème fraîche**
8 **flour tortillas**
75 g (3 oz) **Cheddar cheese**, grated
salt and **pepper**

Salsa verde
500 g (1 lb) **fresh tomatillos** or **green tomatoes**
1 **fresh jalapeño chilli**, deseeded, if liked
1 **fresh poblano chilli**, deseeded, if liked (or use extra jalapeño)
1 **garlic clove**, peeled and left whole
large handful of **coriander leaves**, chopped

Place the chicken in a large saucepan and cover with cold water. Bring to the boil, then reduce the heat and simmer for 15–20 minutes, or until cooked through.

Meanwhile, make the salsa verde. Cook the tomatillos, chillies and garlic under a preheated hot grill for 5–10 minutes, turning frequently, until softened and charred. Leave to cool slightly, then remove the blackened skin.

Remove the chicken from the pan, reserving the cooking liquid. Shred the meat with a fork, discarding the bone.

Place the salsa verde vegetables in a food processor with the coriander and a little of the reserved cooking liquid and whizz to a sauce. Season and set aside.

Mix together the shredded chicken, chorizo and crème fraîche in a bowl, then season.

Divide the chicken mixture among the tortillas, then roll up and place seam-side down in a baking dish. Scatter over the cheese and bake in the oven for 20 minutes until heated through and the cheese has melted. Drizzle over the salsa verde and serve.

For chicken enchiladas with red sauce, make the recipe as above, omitting the salsa verde. To make red sauce, heat 1 tablespoon olive oil in a frying pan, add 1 finely chopped shallot and cook for 3 minutes until softened. Stir in 1 crushed garlic clove and cook for a further 30 seconds. Add a 400 g (13 oz) can chopped tomatoes, a pinch of dried oregano and 1 teaspoon chipotle paste, season and simmer for 10 minutes.

mexican paella

Serves **4–6**
Preparation time **25 minutes**
Cooking time **30–35 minutes**

5 **plum tomatoes**
2 **fresh jalapeño chillies**,
    deseeded, if liked
3 **garlic cloves**, peeled and
    left whole
small handful of **coriander**,
    chopped, plus extra to
    garnish
600 ml (1 pint) **fish stock**
500 g (1 lb) **live clams**,
    cleaned (discard any that
    don't shut when tapped)
150 g (5 oz) **sea bass fillet**,
    cut into bite-sized pieces
1 **squid tube**, cleaned and cut
    into rings
2 tablespoons **olive oil**
1 **onion**, finely chopped
250 g (8 oz) **paella** or other
    short-grain rice
2 tablespoons **tequila**
    (optional)
salt and **pepper**
lime wedges

Cook the tomatoes under a preheated hot grill for 5 minutes until starting to char. Turn the tomatoes over, add the chillies and cook for a further 3 minutes. Turn the chillies over and add the garlic. Continue to cook for 2–3 minutes, turning the garlic once, until softened and charred. Leave to cool slightly, then transfer to a food processor or blender with any juices and the coriander and whizz to a coarse paste. Season and set aside.

Meanwhile, bring the stock to the boil in a saucepan, then reduce the heat and add the clams. Cook for 3–5 minutes until they have opened. Remove from the pan and set aside, discarding any that remain closed. Add the fish to the pan and cook for 2–3 minutes until just opaque, then remove. Add the squid and cook for 1 minute until just cooked through, then remove. Reserve the stock.

Heat the oil in a large frying pan, add the onion and cook for 5 minutes until softened. Stir in the rice, then add the tomato sauce. Pour in the reserved stock (adding 2 times the volume of the rice) and simmer for 12 minutes until most of the liquid has been absorbed.

Arrange the seafood on top of the rice, cover and cook over a low heat for 5–10 minutes until the rice is tender and the seafood is piping hot. Drizzle over the tequila, if using, and scatter over extra coriander and lime wedges.

For vegetarian paella, make the tomato sauce as above. Cook the onion and rice as above, then add the tomato sauce and 600 ml (1 pint) hot vegetable stock and simmer for 12 minutes. Stir in 125 g (4 oz) sweetcorn kernels, 150 g (5 oz) soya beans and a handful of halved cherry tomatoes, cover and continue as above.

blackened chicken & beans

Serves **4**

Preparation time **30 minutes**

Cooking time **40 minutes**

4 **chicken thighs**

4 **chicken drumsticks**

1 teaspoon **cumin seeds**

1 teaspoon **fennel seeds**

1 teaspoon **dried thyme leaves**

1/4 teaspoon **ground cinnamon**

1/2 teaspoon **smoked paprika**

1 tablespoon **sunflower oil**

1 tablespoon **tomato purée**

1 tablespoon **vinegar**

2 tablespoons **dark muscovado sugar**

2 tablespoons **pineapple juice** (from can below)

Bean salad

227 g (7 1/2 oz) can **pineapple in juice**, juice reserved, **pineapple** chopped

400 g (13 oz) can **black-eyed beans**, rinsed and drained

small bunch of **coriander**, roughly chopped

1/2 **red onion**, finely chopped

1 **red pepper**, cored, deseeded and diced

grated rind and juice of **1 lime**

Slash the chicken joints 2–3 times with a knife, then place in a roasting tin. Roughly crush the seeds, then mix together with the next 9 ingredients and spoon over the chicken.

Add 4 tablespoons water to the base of the roasting tin, then place in a preheated oven, 180°C (350°F), Gas Mark 4, for 40 minutes, spooning the pan juices over occasionally until the chicken is deep brown and the juices run clear when the chicken is pierced with a sharp knife.

Meanwhile, make the bean salad. Pour the remaining canned pineapple juice into a bowl and add the chopped pineapple and all the remaining ingredients. Mix together, then serve spoonfuls with the cooked chicken.

For blackened chicken with rice & peas, make the recipe as above, omitting the bean salad. Bring 1 litre (1 3/4 pints) chicken stock and a 400 ml (14 fl oz) can low-fat coconut milk to the boil in a saucepan. Add 200 g (7 oz) long-grain white rice, that has been rinsed with cold water and drained, and a rinsed and drained 400 g (13 oz) can red kidney beans. Simmer for 8 minutes, add 125 g (4 oz) frozen peas and top up with extra boiling water. Cook for 2 minutes, then serve with the chicken.

seared tuna & avocado cups

Serves **4**
Preparation time **15 minutes**,
   plus cooling
Cooking time **15 minutes**

2 tablespoons **olive oil**
4 small **corn tortillas**
4 **tuna steaks**, about 100 g
   (3½ oz) each
1 tablespoon **cumin seeds**
2 **avocados**
100 g (3½ oz) **cherry
   tomatoes**, quartered
1 tablespoon finely chopped
   red onion
handful of **coriander leaves**,
   chopped
grated rind and juice of **1 lime**,
   halved
salt and **pepper**

Brush a little of the oil very lightly over the tortillas, then drape each one over a small ovenproof bowl or ramekin. Place on a baking sheet and bake in a preheated oven, 200°C (400°F), Gas Mark 6, for 5 minutes. Check the tortillas are still centred on the bowls, repositioning them if they have slipped, then cook for a further 5 minutes, or until golden and crisp. Leave to cool.

Rub the remaining oil over the tuna steaks. Press the cumin seeds into the steaks, then season well. Heat a griddle pan until smoking hot, add the tuna and cook for 2–3 minutes on each side until charred but still pink in the centre.

Meanwhile, stone, peel and slice the avocados, then toss together with the tomato, red onion, coriander and a squeeze of lime juice.

Cut the tuna into cubes and pile into the tortilla cups. Top with the avocado mixture, another squeeze of lime juice and a sprinkling of lime rind. Serve immediately.

For grilled tuna & avocado sandwich, cook the tuna as above. Meanwhile, place the stoned and peeled avocados, the tomato, coriander, ½ chopped red chilli (deseeded, if liked) and a squeeze of lime juice in a food processor or blender and whizz to a coarse paste. Lightly toast 4 sandwich rolls. Spread the avocado paste over the rolls, then top with the tuna steaks and serve.

spicy crab pasta

Serves **4**

Preparation time **15 minutes**

Cooking time **45 minutes**

500 g (1 lb) **tomatoes**

2 **garlic cloves**, peeled and left whole

1 tablespoon **chipotle paste**

5 tablespoons **olive oil**

400 g (13 oz) **vermicelli pasta nests**

1 **shallot**, finely chopped

500 ml (17 fl oz) **chicken** or **vegetable stock**

300 g (10 oz) **fresh white crab meat**

salt and **pepper**

lime wedges, to serve

Place the tomatoes in a grill pan and cook under a preheated hot grill for 10 minutes, turning once. Add the garlic and cook for a further 3–5 minutes until softened and charred. Leave to cool slightly, then transfer to a food processor or blender, add the chipotle paste and whizz to a coarse paste. Season and set aside.

Heat the oil in a large frying pan, add the pasta nests and cook for 1–2 minutes until starting to brown, then turn the pasta over and cook for a further 1 minute. Remove from the pan.

Add the shallot to the pan and cook for 3 minutes until softened, then add the tomato sauce and stock. Bring to the boil, then reduce the heat and simmer for 15 minutes.

Return the pasta to the pan and cook gently, stirring frequently, until the pasta is tender and most of the liquid has been absorbed.

Spoon the pasta on to serving plates and scatter over the crab meat. Serve with lime wedges.

For courgette & chorizo pasta, make the tomato sauce and fry the pasta as above. Add 125 g (4 oz) chopped chorizo sausage to the pan and cook for 3 minutes until golden, then remove from pan and set aside. Add the shallot to the pan and cook as above, then stir in 1 chopped courgette and cook for a further 1–2 minutes. Return the chorizo and pasta to the pan with the tomato sauce and stock and continue as above, omitting the crab.

chicken mole

Serves **4**
Preparation time **15 minutes**
Cooking time **50 minutes**

1 tablespoon **sunflower oil**
500 g (1 lb) **minced chicken**
1 **onion**, roughly chopped
2 **garlic cloves**, finely chopped
1 teaspoon **smoked paprika**
½ teaspoon **dried chilli seeds**
1 teaspoon **cumin seeds**,
    roughly crushed
400 g (13 oz) can **chopped
    tomatoes**
400 g (13 oz) can **red kidney
    beans**, rinsed and drained
150 ml (¼ pint) **chicken stock**
1 tablespoon **dark brown
    sugar**
50 g (2 oz) **plain dark
    chocolate**, diced
salt and **pepper**

Heat the oil in a saucepan, add the chicken and onion and cook until browned, breaking up the mince with a wooden spoon. Mix in the garlic, paprika, chilli and cumin and cook for 1 minute.

Stir in the tomatoes, beans, stock and sugar, then mix in the chocolate and season. Cover and simmer gently for 45 minutes, stirring occasionally. Spoon into bowls and serve with the mole toppings (see below).

For mole toppings, to serve as accompaniments, mix together ½ finely chopped red onion, ½ cored, deseeded and diced red pepper, 1 stoned, peeled and diced avocado, the rind and juice of 1 lime and a small bunch of roughly chopped coriander, then spoon into a serving bowl. Place 100 g (3½ oz) tortilla chips in a second bowl and 100 g (3½ oz) grated mature Cheddar cheese in a third. Allow guests to add their own combination of toppings to the mole.

tomato & citrus baked fish

Serves **4**
Preparation time **10 minutes**
Cooking time **15 minutes**

2 tablespoons **olive oil**
4 **halibut steaks**
150 g (5 oz) **cherry tomatoes**, halved
1 **red chilli**, deseeded, if liked, and chopped
grated rind and juice of ½ **orange**
grated rind and juice of 1 **lime**
salt and **pepper**
handful of **coriander leaves**, chopped, to garnish

Rub 1 tablespoon of the oil over the fish and place in a shallow baking tray. Season well.

Scatter the tomatoes and chilli, orange rind and lime rind over the top of each steak. Squeeze over the fruit juices and then drizzle with the remaining oil.

Bake in a preheated oven, 220°C (425°F), Gas Mark 7, for 15 minutes, or until the fish is just cooked through. Serve sprinkled with the chopped coriander.

For halibut steaks in spicy tomato sauce, heat 2 tablespoons olive oil in a deep frying pan, add 1 finely chopped onion and cook for 5 minutes until softened. Add 2 crushed garlic cloves and 1 chopped red chilli (deseeded, if liked) and cook for a further 30 seconds. Stir in a 400 g (13 oz) can chopped tomatoes and the grated rind of ½ orange and simmer for 15 minutes, topping up with water if necessary. Add the halibut steaks to the pan, cover with a lid or foil and continue to cook for 15 minutes, or until the fish is just cooked through. Serve sprinkled with chopped coriander.

baked eggs with chorizo

Serves **4**

Preparation time **10 minutes**

Cooking time **30–35 minutes**

5 **tomatoes**

2 **red chillies**, deseeded, if liked

1 **garlic clove**, peeled and left whole

75 ml (3 fl oz) **water**

½ teaspoon **dried oregano**

1 tablespoon **olive oil**

125 g (4 oz) **chorizo sausage**, chopped

4 **eggs**

salt and **pepper**

4 **corn tortillas**, to serve

Place the tomatoes in a grill pan and cook under a preheated hot grill for 5 minutes until starting to char. Turn the tomatoes over, then add the chillies and cook for a further 5–10 minutes, turning frequently, until they are softened and charred. Leave to cool slightly, then transfer to a food processor or blender, add the garlic and measurement water and whizz to a chunky sauce. Season well and add the dried oregano.

Heat the oil in a small frying pan, add the chorizo and cook for 2 minutes, stirring frequently. Add the tomato sauce and cook for 5 minutes until slightly thickened. Divide the sauce among 4 individual ramekins, then crack an egg into each one.

Place the ramekins on a baking sheet and bake in a preheated oven, 200°C (400°F), Gas Mark 6, for 12 minutes, or until the eggs are just set. Serve with corn tortillas.

For thick Mexican omelette, heat 2 tablespoons olive oil in a large frying pan, add 125 g (4 oz) sliced chorizo and cook until crisp. Add 1 sliced garlic clove and cook for a further 30 seconds. Reduce the heat, pour in 8 beaten eggs and scatter over 75 g (3 oz) sliced cherry tomatoes and 1 sliced green chilli (deseeded, if liked), then cook for 10 minutes until set. Scatter over 25 g (1 oz) crumbled feta cheese and a little chopped coriander to serve.

tuna steaks with green salsa

Serves **4**

Preparation time **14 minutes**, plus marinating

Cooking time **2–4 minutes**

2 tablespoons **olive oil**

grated rind of 1 **lemon**

2 teaspoons chopped **parsley**

½ teaspoon crushed **coriander seeds**

4 **tuna steaks**, about 150 g (5 oz) each

salt and **pepper**

Salsa

2 tablespoons chopped **capers**

2 tablespoons chopped **cornichons**

1 tablespoon finely chopped **parsley**

2 teaspoons chopped **chives**

2 teaspoons finely chopped **chervil**

30 g (1½ oz) pitted **green olives**, chopped

1 **shallot**, finely chopped (optional)

2 tablespoons **lemon juice**

2 tablespoons **olive oil**

Mix together the oil, lemon rind, parsley and coriander seeds with plenty of pepper in a bowl, then rub over the tuna steaks.

Make the salsa by mixing together all the ingredients in a bowl. Season to taste and set aside.

Heat a griddle or frying pan until smoking hot, add the tuna and cook for 1–2 minutes on each side until well seared but still pink in the centre. Remove from the pan and leave to rest for a couple of minutes.

Serve the tuna steaks with a spoonful of the salsa, a dressed salad and plenty of fresh crusty bread.

For yellow pepper & mustard salsa, to replace the green salsa, mix together 2 cored, deseeded and finely chopped yellow peppers, 1 tablespoon Dijon mustard, 2 tablespoons each of finely chopped chives, parsley and dill, 1 teaspoon sugar, 1 tablespoon cider vinegar and 2 tablespoons olive oil in a bowl. Make the recipe as above and serve with the salsa.

spiced pork with pineapple salsa

Serves **4**

Preparation time **20 minutes**,
plus soaking and marinating

Cooking time **25 minutes**

3 **dried ancho chillies**, stems
removed and deseeded

3 **cloves**

4 **allspice berries**

½ teaspoon **cumin seeds**

½ **cinnamon stick**

2 teaspoons **dried oregano**

1 tablespoon **red wine
vinegar**

2 **garlic cloves**, chopped

2 teaspoons **clear honey**

1 tablespoon **olive oil**

2 small **pork tenderloins**,
about 300 g (11 oz) each
(or 1 large, about 450 g/1 lb)

salt and **pepper**

Salsa

½ ripe **pineapple**, skinned,
cored and chopped

1 tablespoon finely chopped
red onion

1 **red chilli**, deseeded, if liked,
and chopped

juice of ½ **lime**

handful of **coriander leaves**,
chopped

Heat a dry nonstick frying pan until hot, add the chillies
and dry-fry for 1 minute on each side until lightly toasted.
Transfer to a heatproof bowl, pour over boiling water to
cover and leave to soak for 30 minutes until softened.

Add the whole spices to the pan and cook for 30
seconds until they emit an aroma. Tip into a pestle and
mortar or spice grinder and grind until finely ground.

Remove the chillies from the soaking liquid, add to
a mini processor or blender with the spices, oregano,
vinegar, garlic, honey and oil and whizz to a smooth
paste. Rub all over the pork in a shallow non-metallic
dish, cover with clingfilm and leave to marinate in the
refrigerator for 2 hours.

Wipe away any excess marinade from the pork, then
place in a shallow baking tray and season. Bake in
a preheated oven, 200°C (400°F), Gas Mark 6, for
25 minutes until just cooked through.

Meanwhile, make the salsa by mixing together all the
ingredients in a bowl, then season.

Cut the pork into thick slices and serve with the salsa.

For spicy pork chops with pineapple, mix together
½ teaspoon ground cumin, 1–2 tablespoons chipotle
paste and 1 tablespoon olive oil in a bowl, then rub
all over 4 large pork chops. Cook the chops under a
preheated hot grill for 7 minutes. Turn the chops over
and cook for a further 3 minutes. Place 1 pineapple
ring on top of each chop and continue to cook for
5 minutes, or until the pork is cooked through and the
pineapple caramelized.

swiss chard & tomato tamales

Serves **4**

Preparation time **30 minutes**,
  plus soaking and cooling

Cooking time
  1 hour 10 minutes

8 **corn husks** (or use
  greaseproof paper and foil as
  for Cheesy Swiss Chard &
  Chicken Tamales below)
1 tablespoon **olive oil**
1 **onion**, finely chopped
large bunch of **Swiss chard**,
  leaves separated and stalks
  finely chopped
2 **garlic cloves**, finely chopped
1 **fresh jalapeño chilli**,
  deseeded, if liked, and
  chopped
1 **tomato**, chopped
150 ml (¼ pint) **crème fraîche**
300 g (10 oz) **masa harina** or
  fine cornmeal
1 teaspoon **baking powder**
1 teaspoon **salt**
3 tablespoons **lard**
500 ml (17 fl oz) warm
  vegetable stock

Soak the corn husks in plenty of warm water for
10 minutes until pliable, then drain.

Heat the oil in a frying pan, add the onion and cook
for 5 minutes until softened. Add the chard stalks and
cook for 3 minutes until softened. Add the chard leaves,
garlic, chilli and tomato and cook for a further 1 minute.
Stir in the crème fraiche and leave to bubble until it just
coats the vegetables. Leave to cool.

Meanwhile, beat together the masa harina, baking
powder, salt and lard in a bowl, then beat in the stock
until a soft dough forms.

Lay out 1 corn husk so it is flat, place a spoonful of the
dough in the centre and down towards the bottom of
the husk, then flatten with your hand. Place a spoonful
of the chard mixture on top, then fold over the husk so
the filling is tightly enclosed and forms a cylinder. Leave
the top end open and secure with strips of leftover husk.
Repeat with the remaining ingredients.

Place the parcels, sealed end down, into a steamer.
Cover and steam for about 1 hour, until the dough
comes away easily from the husk.

For cheesy Swiss chard & chicken tamales, make
the recipe as above, omitting the corn husks and
replacing the crème fraîche with 1 ready-cooked and
shredded chicken breast and 150 g (5 oz) mozzarella
cheese. Cut out 8 pieces of greaseproof or nonstick
baking paper and 8 pieces of foil, about 10 x 20 cm
(4 x 8 inches). Place the paper pieces on top of the foil
pieces. Make up the parcels as above, using the paper
and foil wrappers in place of the husks. Steam as above.

poached sea bass & salsa

Serves **4**
Preparation time **15 minutes**
Cooking time **25 minutes**

5 cm (2 inch) piece of **fresh root ginger**, peeled and thinly sliced
2 **lemon grass stalks**, sliced lengthways
1 **lime**, sliced
200 ml (7 fl oz) **dry sherry**
2 tablespoons **fish sauce**
2 **sea bass**, about 625 g (1¼ lb) each, cleaned and scaled
lime wedges, to serve

Salsa

3 firm **tomatoes**, deseeded and finely diced
1 **lemon grass stalk**, outer leaves discarded, finely chopped
1 teaspoon peeled and finely grated **fresh root ginger**
2 tablespoons chopped **coriander leaves**
2 **spring onions**, finely chopped
2 teaspoons **groundnut oil**
1 tablespoon **lime juice**
1½ teaspoons **light soy sauce**

Place the sliced ginger, sliced lemon grass, lime slices, sherry, fish sauce and enough water to just cover the fish in a fish kettle or large frying pan. Bring to the boil, then reduce the heat and simmer gently for 5 minutes.

Add the sea bass to the fish kettle or place on a large piece of nonstick baking paper if using a frying pan. Lower into the stock, adding more water if necessary so that it covers the fish. Bring the stock to the boil and then turn off the heat. Cover and leave to poach for 15 minutes, or until the fish flakes easily when pressed in the centre with a knife.

Meanwhile, make the salsa. Place the tomatoes, finely chopped lemon grass, grated ginger, coriander and spring onions in a bowl. Stir in the oil, lime juice and soy sauce and leave to infuse.

Lift the poached sea bass carefully out of the cooking liquid and on to a plate. Peel away the skin and gently lift the fillets from the bones. Place on a serving dish with the salsa and lime wedges. Serve with steamed rice, if liked.

For pan-fried sea bass with salsa, ask the fishmonger to fillet the whole sea bass. Heat 1 tablespoon olive oil in a nonstick frying pan and pan-fry the sea bass fillets over a medium-high heat, skin-side down, for 3–4 minutes. Reduce the heat, cover and cook for a further 3–4 minutes, or until cooked through. Meanwhile, make the salsa as above, then serve with the cooked fish.

roast chicken with smoky sauce

Serves **4–6**

Preparation time **15 minutes**

Cooking time
  1 hour 20 minutes

100 ml (3½ fl oz) **olive oil**

1 whole **chicken**, about 1.5 kg
  (3½ lb)

150 g (5 oz) **chorizo
  sausage**, chopped

1 **onion**, finely chopped

300 g (10 oz) **cornbread**, torn
  into large chunks

200 ml (7 fl oz) hot **chicken
  stock**

2 **fresh jalapeño** or **poblano
  chillies**, deseeded, if liked

1 tablespoon chopped **shallot**

juice of ½ **lime**

50 g (2 oz) **spinach leaves**

large handful of **coriander
  leaves**

2 teaspoons **honey**

salt and **pepper**

Rub a little of the oil over the chicken and season well. Place in a shallow baking dish and roast in a preheated oven, 190°C (375°F), Gas Mark 5, for 20 minutes, then a further 20 minutes per pound, or until the juices run clear when the thickest part of the chicken thigh is pierced with a sharp knife.

Meanwhile, heat 1 tablespoon of the oil in a frying pan, add the chorizo and cook for 3 minutes until lightly crisp, then transfer to a bowl. Add the onion to the pan and cook for 5 minutes until softened. Add the onion and cornbread to the chorizo and mix together, then place in a lightly greased medium-sized baking dish. Pour over the stock, cover with foil and bake in the oven with the chicken for 10 minutes, then remove the foil and cook for a further 10 minutes, or until crispy on top.

Rub a little oil over the chillies, then cook under a preheated hot grill for 5 minutes, turning frequently, until charred. Place in a plastic food bag, seal and leave for 5 minutes until cool enough to handle. When cool, peel away the blackened skin and remove the seeds and membrane. Place the flesh in a food processor or blender with 5 tablespoons of the oil and the remaining ingredients and whizz until smooth, then season. Serve with the roast chicken and stuffing.

scallops with mango salsa

Serves **4**

Preparation time **15 minutes**, plus cooling

Cooking time **15 minutes**

200 ml (7 fl oz) **mango juice**

25 g (1 oz) **dried mango**, finely chopped

½ teaspoon peeled and finely chopped **fresh root ginger**

1 tablespoon **olive oil**

12 plump **scallops**, patted dry with kitchen paper

1 **mango**, peeled, stoned and chopped

2 **spring onions**, sliced

1 **red chilli**, deseeded, if liked, and chopped

grated rind and juice of **1 lime**

handful of **coriander leaves**

salt and **pepper**

mixed salad leaves, to serve

Place the mango juice, dried mango and ginger in a small saucepan and bring to the boil, then cook for about 5 minutes until reduced by half. Transfer the mixture to a bowl and leave to cool.

Heat a nonstick frying pan until smoking, add the oil then the scallops and cook for 3 minutes on each side until golden and just cooked through.

Meanwhile, mix together the cooled mango mixture and the remaining ingredients, then season.

Spoon the salsa over the scallops and serve with the salad leaves.

For seared tuna with mango salsa, make the salsa as above. Brush 1 tablespoon olive oil over a 400 g (13 oz) thick tuna steak. Mix together 1 teaspoon each of roughly ground coriander seeds and cumin seeds and press all over the tuna. Wrap very tightly in a piece of foil. Heat a dry frying pan until smoking hot, add the tuna parcel and cook for 7 minutes, turning frequently, until evenly cooked but still pink in the centre. Leave to cool slightly, then unwrap and slice and serve with the salsa.

134

red mole with pulled pork

Serves **6**

Preparation time **25 minutes**, plus soaking

Cooking time **2 hours 10 minutes**

1 teaspoon **tomato purée**

500 ml (17 fl oz) hot **vegetable stock**

875 g (1¾ lb) **pork shoulder**, cut into large fist-sized pieces

1 **cinnamon stick**

3 **dried ancho chillies**, stems removed and deseeded

1 **onion**, halved

5 large **tomatoes**, halved

4 **garlic cloves**, peeled and left whole

3–4 tablespoons **lard** or **vegetable oil**

50 g (2 oz) **blanched almonds**

50 g (2 oz) **raisins**

1 teaspoon **ground cumin**

½ teaspoon **dried oregano**

25 g (1 oz) **plain dark chocolate**, chopped

salt and **pepper**

Mix together the tomato purée and stock in a jug. Place the pork in a large saucepan and cover with the stock. Add the cinnamon stick and bring to the boil, then reduce the heat and simmer for 1½ hours, or until the pork is cooked through. Remove the pork from the stock, reserving the liquid. Use a fork to shred the meat.

Meanwhile, heat a nonstick frying pan until hot, add the chillies and dry-fry for 1 minute on each side until they start to crackle. Remove the pan from the heat, pour in boiling water to cover and leave to soak for 30 minutes.

Cook the onion and tomatoes under a preheated hot grill for 7 minutes. Turn them over and add the garlic, then cook for a further 5–7 minutes until softened and lightly charred. Transfer to a food processor or blender.

Heat 2–3 tablespoons of the lard or oil in a frying pan, add the almonds and cook for 3 minutes until lightly browned, then tip into the blender. Add the raisins to the pan and cook for 1 minute, or until puffed. Drain the chillies and add to the blender with the raisins and 200 ml (7 fl oz) of the pork cooking liquid. Whizz until smooth.

Add a little more lard to the frying pan, pour in the tomato sauce and cook for 5 minutes, stirring continuously, until thickened. Add the cumin, oregano and chocolate, top up with more cooking liquid, then simmer for 30 minutes. Stir the pork into the sauce and cook for a further 5 minutes. Serve with warm tortillas and salsa (see below).

For radish salsa, thinly slice 150 g (5 oz) radishes. Toss together with the grated rind and juice of ½ lime and some chopped coriander leaves. Season well.

seared salmon and avocado salad

Serves **4**
Preparation time **15 minutes**
Cooking time **6 minutes**

2 tablespoons **olive oil**
4 pieces of **salmon fillet**,
    about 200 g (7 oz) each, skin
    on and pin-boned
1 large **orange**, halved
2 tablespoons **extra virgin
    olive oil**
salt and **pepper**

Avocado salad
2 ripe **avocados**
1 **red chilli**, deseeded, if liked,
    and finely chopped
juice of 1 **lime**
1 tablespoon roughly chopped
    coriander leaves
1 tablespoon **olive oil**

Heat a frying pan over a high heat until hot, then add the 2 tablespoons olive oil. Season the salmon and place it, skin-side down, in the pan. Cook for 4 minutes, then turn the fish over and cook for a further 2 minutes.

Meanwhile, heat a separate small dry frying pan until hot, add the orange halves, cut-side down, and sear until starting to char. Remove the oranges from the pan and squeeze the juice back into the pan. Bring the juice to the boil and reduce it to about 1 tablespoon. Whisk in the extra virgin olive oil, then season.

Make the salad. Stone and peel the avocados, then cut into 1 cm (½ inch) dice and place in a mixing bowl. Add the remaining ingredients and season.

Spoon the salad into the centre of each plate. Place a piece of salmon on top and drizzle with the burnt orange vinaigrette.

For salmon with orange couscous, pan-fry 4 salmon steaks as above. Bring 400 ml (14 fl oz) freshly squeezed orange juice and 2 tablespoons raisins to the boil in a saucepan. Place 300 g (10 oz) couscous in a heatproof bowl and pour over the orange juice. Cover the bowl with clingfilm and leave the couscous to steam for 5 minutes before fluffing up the grains with a fork. Add 1 tablespoon olive oil, a large handful of chopped coriander leaves and 2 tablespoons pine nuts. Serve with crème fraîche and the warm salmon.

steak with roasted pepper sauce

Serves **4**

Preparation time **15 minutes**

Cooking time **20–25 minutes**

4 **plum tomatoes**, halved

1 **red pepper**, cored,
deseeded and halved

1 **shallot**, thickly sliced

2 **garlic cloves**, peeled and
left whole

squeeze of **lime juice**

3 tablespoons **olive oil**

1 **red onion**, thickly sliced

1 teaspoon **ground cumin**

4 **ribeye steaks**, about 125 g
(4 oz) each

salt and **pepper**

To serve

25 g (1 oz) **feta cheese**,
crumbled

soft **polenta**

Cook the tomatoes, red pepper, shallot and garlic cloves under a preheated hot grill for 10 minutes, turning frequently, until softened and lightly charred. Leave to cool slightly then peel away the skin from the pepper. Place the roasted vegetables in a food processor or blender, add the lime juice and whizz together. Season and set aside.

Rub 1 tablespoon of the oil over the red onion, sprinkle over the cumin and season. Heat a griddle pan until smoking, then add the onion and cook for 5 minutes, turning frequently, until soft and charred. Remove from the pan and keep warm.

Brush the remaining oil over the steaks and season well. Add to the pan and cook for 2–3 minutes on each side until browned and cooked to your liking. Transfer the steaks and onions to serving plates, drizzle over the sauce and scatter with the feta. Serve with soft polenta.

For chilli potato gratin, to serve as an accompaniment, rub a little oil over 2 fresh poblano chillies, then cook under a preheated hot grill for 5–7 minutes, turning frequently, until charred. Place in a plastic food bag. When cool enough to handle, remove the skin, seeds and membrane, then slice the flesh and set aside. Thinly slice 1 kg (2 lb) potatoes, then pat dry. Place 300 ml (½ pint) double cream, 300 ml (½ pint) milk and 1 finely chopped shallot in a saucepan and bring just to the boil, then simmer for 5 minutes. Season, then strain. Lay half the potatoes in a lightly buttered baking dish. Pour over half the milk mixture and chilli strips. Arrange the remaining potato on top, pour over the milk and top with more chilli. Bake in a preheated oven, 180°C (350°F), Gas Mark 4, for 45 minutes, or until soft and lightly browned.

chicken with pumpkin seeds

Serves **4**

Preparation time **10 minutes**, plus cooling

Cooking time **30 minutes**

75 g (3 oz) **pumpkin seeds**

1 small **onion**, chopped

1 **green chilli**, deseeded, if liked, and chopped

½ teaspoon **dried oregano**

large handful of **coriander leaves**, including the stalks

200 ml (7 fl oz) **chicken stock**

2 tablespoons **olive oil**

4 skinless, boneless **chicken breasts**, about 125 g (4 oz) each

salt and **pepper**

handful of sliced **radishes**, to serve

Heat a large, dry nonstick frying pan until hot, add the pumpkin seeds and dry-fry for 3–5 minutes, stirring frequently, until golden and starting to pop. Leave to cool.

When cool, place the pumpkin seeds in a food processor or blender with the onion, chilli, oregano, coriander and 75 ml (3 fl oz) of the stock and whizz to a smooth paste.

Heat 1 tablespoon of the oil in a saucepan, add the paste and cook for about 10 minutes, stirring frequently, until thickened. Pour in the remaining stock and simmer for 15 minutes.

Meanwhile, rub the remaining oil over the chicken, then season. Heat a griddle pan until smoking hot, add the chicken and cook for 5–7 minutes on each side until just cooked through. Cut into slices and arrange on a serving plate with the radishes. Serve with the sauce spooned over.

For pumpkin-seed-crusted chicken, place 100 g (3½ oz) pumpkin seeds in a food processor or blender and whizz until small pieces form. Transfer to a bowl and stir in 75 g (3 oz) dried breadcrumbs and 1 teaspoon ground cumin. Place 50 g (2 oz) plain flour on a plate, 1 beaten egg on a second plate and the pumpkin seed mixture on a third. Place the chicken breasts between 2 sheets of clingfilm and lightly pound with a rolling pin until 1 cm (½ inch) or less thick. Dip each flattened breast in the flour, then the egg and finally the pumpkin seed mixture, letting any excess drip away. Season. Heat 2 tablespoons olive oil in a large frying pan, add the chicken breasts and cook for 5 minutes on each side, or until golden and cooked through.

prawn & sweetcorn tacos

Serves **4**

Preparation time **20 minutes**, plus cooling

Cooking time **20 minutes**

1 tablespoon **olive oil**

2 **corn on the cobs**, husks removed

8 large **corn tortillas**

150 ml (¼ pint) **soured cream**

½ teaspoon **chilli powder**

200 g (7 oz) large ready-cooked **peeled prawns** (tails can be left on)

1 **spring onion**, sliced

½ **iceberg lettuce**, finely sliced

Red pepper salsa

3 tablespoons **olive oil**

1 **red pepper**

grated rind and juice of ½ **lime**

handful of **coriander leaves**, chopped

salt and **pepper**

Make the salsa. Rub 1 tablespoon of the oil over the red pepper, then cook under a preheated hot grill for 10–12 minutes, turning frequently, until charred. Place in a bowl and cover. When cool enough to handle, peel away the skin, remove the seeds and membrane, then finely chop the flesh. Mix together with the remaining oil, the lime juice, a little lime rind and the coriander. Season. Set aside.

Rub half the oil over the corn cobs. Cook in a hot griddle pan for 3 minutes on each side, then remove from the pan. Using a sharp knife, slice the sweetcorn kernels away from the cobs. Meanwhile, use tongs to hold a tortilla over a gas flame until softened and lightly charred. Repeat with the remaining tortillas.

Mix together the soured cream with the remaining lime rind from the salsa and the chilli powder. Pile the sweetcorn and prawns on to the tortillas. Scatter over the spring onion and lettuce, then top with some red pepper salsa and the chilli soured cream. Serve immediately.

For prawn & sweetcorn skewers, cut 2 corn on the cobs into thick slices and thread on to 8 metal skewers, alternating with 12 large prawns and 1 cored and deseeded red pepper, cut into wedges. Mix together 1 tablespoon olive oil, ½ teaspoon ground cumin and 1 cored, deseeded and finely chopped red pepper in a bowl, then brush all over the skewers. Cook for 3–5 minutes on each side until soft. Meanwhile, mix together 150 ml (¼ pint) soured cream, the grated rind of 1 lime, a little lime juice and a handful of chopped coriander leaves. Serve the skewers with the lime cream.

snapper with chilli tomato sauce

Serves **4**
Preparation time **10 minutes**
Cooking time **30 minutes**

3 tablespoons **olive oil**
1 **onion**, finely chopped
2 **garlic cloves**, crushed
100 ml (3½ fl oz) **dry white wine**
400 g (13 oz) can **chopped tomatoes**
1 tablespoon **capers**, drained
100 g (3½ oz) **pimento-stuffed olives**, drained
1 tablespoon sliced **pickled jalapeño chillies**
½ teaspoon **dried oregano**
4 **red snapper fillets**, about 125 g (4 oz) each
salt and **pepper**
rice, to serve

Heat 2 tablespoons of the oil in a saucepan, add the onion and cook for 5 minutes until softened. Add the garlic and cook for a further 30 seconds. Pour in the wine and simmer for 1–2 minutes until reduced by half.

Add the tomatoes, season and bring to the boil, then reduce the heat, add the capers, olives, jalapeño slices and oregano and simmer for 20 minutes, topping up with water if necessary.

Meanwhile, heat the remaining oil in a large nonstick frying pan, add the snapper fillets, skin-side down, and cook for 7 minutes until golden and crisp. Turn the fish over and cook for a further 5 minutes, or until the fish is just cooked through. Spoon over the sauce and serve with rice.

For chicken with chilli tomato sauce, make the sauce as above. Rub 1 tablespoon olive oil over 4 boneless, skinless chicken breasts (about 125 g/ 4 oz each) and season well. Heat a griddle pan, add the chicken and cook for 5 minutes on each side until charred. Add to the sauce and cook for a further 3–5 minutes until the chicken is just cooked through. Serve scattered with parsley leaves.

sides

baked chillies with cheese

Serves **6**
Preparation time **15 minutes**
Cooking time **10–15 minutes**

175 g (6 oz) **cream cheese**
100 g (3½ oz) **goats' cheese**
100 g (3½ oz) **Cheddar
cheese**, grated
2 **spring onions**, sliced
12 fresh **jalapeño chillies**,
deseeded, if liked, and
halved
1 **tomato**, chopped

Place the cheeses in a bowl and mix together until smooth, then gently stir in the spring onions. Spoon a little of the cheese mixture into each chilli half, filling the cavity.

Transfer the chillies to a lightly oiled baking sheet and scatter over the tomato. Bake in a preheated oven, 200°C (400°F), Gas Mark 6, for 10–15 minutes until soft and lightly charred.

For cheesy fried chillies, place the whole chillies under a preheated hot grill and cook for 5 minutes, turning once or twice, until charred. Place in a plastic food bag, seal and leave for 5 minutes until cool enough to handle. Meanwhile, make the cheese mixture as above, omitting the spring onion. Peel away the blackened chilli skin and cut a slit into each chilli, scooping out the seeds. Fill each chilli with the cheese mixture, then secure the openings with cocktail sticks. Whisk 2 egg whites in a clean bowl until soft peaks form. Add 1 egg yolk and a pinch of salt and whisk until combined. Dip each chilli in plain flour, then in the whisked egg, until well coated. Fill a large saucepan one-third full of vegetable oil and heat to 180–190°C (350–375°F), or until a cube of bread browns in 15 seconds. Deep-fry the chillies, in batches, for 2–3 minutes until golden and crisp. Remove with a slotted spoon and drain on kitchen paper.

chilli cornbread

Serves **8**

Preparation time **10 minutes**,
  plus cooling

Cooking time **40 minutes**

100 g (3½ oz) **butter**

1 **onion**, finely chopped

225 g (8 oz) **coarse cornmeal**
  or **polenta**

150 g (5 oz) **plain flour**

1 tablespoon **sugar**

2 teaspoons **baking powder**

1½ teaspoons **salt**

300 ml (10 fl oz) **buttermilk**

2 **eggs**, beaten

2 **red chillies**, 1 finely
  chopped and 1 sliced

125 g (4 oz) **Cheddar
  cheese**, grated

Heat the butter in a small saucepan, add the onion and cook for 5 minutes until softened. Leave to cool slightly.

Tip all the dry ingredients into a large bowl. Mix together the buttermilk and eggs in a jug, then pour into the dry ingredients and mix together until smooth. Add the finely chopped chilli, most of the cheese and the cooked onions and butter mixture, then stir until well combined.

Spoon the mixture into a greased and lined 20 cm (8 inch) deep cake tin or deep ovenproof frying pan. Smooth over the surface with a spoon, then scatter over the sliced chilli.

Bake in a preheated oven, 200°C (400°F), Gas Mark 6, for 25 minutes. Sprinkle over the remaining cheese and return to the oven for a further 10 minutes, or until cooked through. Leave to stand for 2 minutes, then turn out and serve warm.

For bacon & roasted pepper cornbread, cook 3 bacon rashers under a preheated grill until just crisp. Leave to cool, then cut into small strips. Make the chilli cornbread as above, adding the bacon strips and 1 chopped ready-roasted red pepper with the cooked onion.

refried beans

Serves **6**
Preparation time **5 minutes**
Cooking time **15–20 minutes**

5 tablespoons **lard** or
   vegetable oil
1 **onion**, finely chopped
4 **garlic cloves**, crushed
2 x 400 g (13 oz) cans **black
   beans**, drained with liquid
   reserved (for home-cooked
   see below)
½ teaspoon **dried oregano**
salt and **pepper**
50 g (2 oz) **feta cheese**,
   crumbled, to serve

To garnish
coriander leaves, chopped,
½ **red chilli**, deseeded, if liked,
   and chopped

Heat the lard or vegetable oil in a large frying pan, add the onion and cook for 5–10 minutes until golden. Add the garlic and cook for a further 1 minute.

Meanwhile, place the black beans and 2 tablespoons of the reserved bean liquid in a food processor or blender and whizz until smooth.

Add the puréed beans and oregano to the onion mixture, reduce the heat to low and cook for 5 minutes, stirring frequently. Add 100 ml (3½ fl oz) of the reserved bean liquid and cook for a further 5 minutes until the beans are the consistency of very soft mashed potatoes.

Season, sprinkle over the cheese and serve garnished with the coriander and chilli.

For home-cooked beans, rinse 200 g (7 oz) dried black beans. Heat 2 tablespoons lard or vegetable oil in a large saucepan, add 1 sliced onion and cook for 5–10 minutes until soft and golden. Add 2 litres (3½ pints) water, the rinsed beans and 1 oregano sprig or ½ teaspoon dried oregano and bring to the boil. Reduce the heat and simmer, partially covered, for 2 hours, topping up with water if necessary, until the beans are tender.

green rice

Serves **4**
Preparation time **10 minutes**
Cooking time **20 minutes**

1 **shallot**, chopped
1 **green chilli**, deseeded, if
    liked, and finely chopped
1 **garlic clove**
grated rind and juice of 1 **lime**
handful of **parsley**
large handful of **coriander
    leaves**
600 ml (1 pint) **chicken** or
    vegetable stock
2 tablespoons **olive oil**
250 g (8 oz) **basmati rice**
salt and **pepper**

Place the shallot, chilli, garlic, lime rind, herbs and
200 ml (7 fl oz) of the stock in a food processor or
blender and whizz until smooth.

Heat the oil in a large saucepan, add the green sauce
and cook for 3 minutes, stirring frequently. Add the rice
and season, then mix well.

Pour in the remaining stock and bring to the boil, then
boil for 10 minutes until most of the liquid has been
absorbed. Cover with a tight-fitting lid, reduce the heat
to its lowest setting and cook for 5 minutes, or until the
rice is tender. Squeeze over the lime juice to taste just
before serving.

For green rice & vegetables, make the recipe as
above, adding 2 finely grated carrots and 1 large
cubed chayote or 1 large cubed courgette with the
rice. Gently flake the vegetables through the rice just
before serving.

citrus & chilli sweet potato mash

Serves **4**
Preparation time **10 minutes**
Cooking time **50 minutes**

4 large **sweet potatoes**
25 g (1 oz) **butter**
grated rind of 1 **orange**, plus
   1 tablespoon juice
1 teaspoon **chipotle paste**
2 tablespoons **soured cream**
salt and **pepper**

Pierce each potato a couple of times with a skewer and place on a baking sheet. Bake in a preheated oven, 200°C (400°F), Gas Mark 6, for 45 minutes until very soft. Leave until cool enough to handle, then use a spoon to scoop out the flesh.

Heat the butter, orange rind and juice in a saucepan until the butter is melted. Remove from the heat and add the sweet potato flesh and chipotle paste, then mash until smooth. Season well.

Transfer the mash to a serving dish, spoon over the soured cream and serve.

For chilli-topped baked sweet potatoes, bake the sweet potatoes as above, then split them open with a knife. Season well, then drizzle 1 tablespoon soured cream over each potato. Sprinkle with ¼ teaspoon ground cumin and top with 1 finely chopped red chilli (deseeded, if liked) and a handful of chopped coriander leaves.

homemade tortillas

Makes **10**

Preparation time **20 minutes**, plus resting

Cooking time **20 minutes**

300 g (10 oz) **masa harina** or **fine cornmeal**

350 ml (12 fl oz) **warm water**

1 tablespoon **olive oil**

salt

Place the masa harina or cornmeal and a good pinch of salt in a bowl and mix together. Add half the measurement water and leave to stand for 10 minutes. Pour in the remaining water and the oil and mix together to form a soft, smooth dough.

Divide the dough into 10 equal pieces and roll each into a ball. Cover both sides of a tortilla press with clingfilm. Place a ball of dough inside and press down to flatten. Alternatively, place a ball inside a large plastic food bag and either roll out on a work surface or use a heavy-based saucepan to flatten the dough into a round about 1–2 mm (⅛ inch) thick. Repeat with the remaining dough.

Heat a large, dry nonstick frying pan until hot. Peel away the clingfilm from the tortillas, place 1 in the pan and cook for 1 minute on each side until lightly charred. Repeat with the remaining tortillas. Serve with fajitas, fried as chips (see below) or with guacamole (see page 18).

For crispy tortilla chips, cook the tortillas as above and leave to cool slightly, or use ready-made corn tortillas. Cut the tortillas into triangles. Heat a large frying pan, add 5 tablespoons vegetable oil and cook the chips, in batches, for 1–2 minutes on each side until golden and crisp. Serve with salsa or guacamole (see page 18) for dipping.

sweetcorn with herby chilli salt

Serves **4**
Preparation time **5 minutes**
Cooking time **5–10 minutes**

2 teaspoons **olive oil**
4 **corn on the cobs**, husks
    removed
1 teaspoon **sea salt flakes**
handful of **coriander leaves**,
    finely chopped
1 teaspoon **chilli powder**

Rub the oil all over the corn cobs, then cook under a preheated medium grill for 5–10 minutes, turning frequently, until charred all over.

Meanwhile, mix together the salt, coriander and chilli powder in a bowl until well combined.

Sprinkle a little of the chilli salt over each corn cob and serve.

For chilli & cheese grilled sweetcorn, grill the corn on the cobs as above. When the sweetcorn is golden and almost cooked through, scatter over the chilli powder and cook for a further 1–2 minutes. Remove from the heat, scatter over 25 g (1 oz) crumbled feta cheese and serve.

chorizo with red beans

Serves **4**

Preparation time **10 minutes**

Cooking time **20 minutes**

2 tablespoons **olive oil**

125 g (4 oz) **chorizo sausage**, sliced

1 small **onion**, finely chopped

2 **garlic cloves**, crushed

1 teaspoon **tomato purée**

2 **tomatoes**, chopped

400 g (13 oz) can **pinto** or **kidney beans**, including the liquid

salt and **pepper**

handful of **coriander leaves**, chopped, to garnish

lime wedges, to serve

Heat 1 tablespoon of the oil in a heavy-based saucepan, add the chorizo and cook for 3 minutes, turning occasionally, until lightly browned all over. Remove from the pan and set aside.

Add the remaining oil to the pan, add the onion and cook for 5 minutes until softened. Stir in the garlic and tomato purée, add the tomatoes and season. Cook for a couple of minutes until the tomatoes start to soften.

Tip in the beans and the liquid, and top up with a little water if necessary. Return the chorizo to the pan and simmer for 10 minutes. Scatter over the coriander and serve with lime wedges for squeezing over.

For bean bites, drain a 400 g (13 oz) can pinto beans, then lightly mash. Mix together with 1 teaspoon ground cumin, a handful of chopped coriander leaves and 2 sliced spring onions. Season, then shape into 8 small patties. Dust each one in plain flour, dip in 1 beaten egg, letting the excess drip away, then press into 100 g (3½ oz) dried breadcrumbs until coated all over. Heat 4 tablespoons olive oil in a large frying pan, add the patties and cook for 5–10 minutes until golden all over. Serve with lime wedges for squeezing over.

creamy chilli mushrooms

Serves **4**
Preparation time **5 minutes**
Cooking time **5–10 minutes**

1 tablespoon **olive oil**
250 g (8 oz) **mixed mushrooms**
2 **garlic cloves**, sliced
75 g (3 oz) **cherry tomatoes**, halved
1 teaspoon **chipotle paste**
50 ml (2 fl oz) **crème fraîche**
salt and **pepper**

Heat the oil in a large frying pan, add the mushrooms and cook for 3 minutes until starting to soften. Stir in the garlic and tomatoes, season and cook for a further 1 minute.

Stir in the chipotle paste and crème fraîche and let it bubble for 1–2 minutes. Serve immediately.

For Mexican mushroom & sweetcorn salsa, heat 1 tablespoon olive oil in a frying pan, add 1 cored, deseeded and finely chopped red pepper and cook for 1 minute until starting to soften. Add 150 g (5 oz) canned huitlacoche or other mushrooms and heat through. Stir in 50 g (2 oz) canned sweetcorn and leave to cool. When ready to serve, stir in lime juice to taste, 1 chopped red chilli, a handful of chopped coriander leaves and 1 sliced spring onion.

roasted squash

Serves **4**
Preparation time **10 minutes**
Cooking time **35–40 minutes**

500 g (1 lb) **butternut** or other
   squash, deseeded and cut
   into 2 cm (¾ inch) thick
   slices
2 tablespoons **olive oil**
1 **red chilli**, deseeded, if liked,
   and sliced
2 tablespoons **pumpkin
   seeds**
salt and **pepper**

Toss the squash with the oil, season well and place on a baking sheet. Roast in a preheated oven, 220°C (425°F), Gas Mark 7, for 20 minutes.

Turn the slices over, return to the oven and cook for a further 10 minutes. Scatter over the chilli and pumpkin seeds, return to the oven and continue to cook for 5–10 minutes until soft.

For roasted squash & red pepper with coriander pesto, cook the squash for 20 minutes as above, then add 1 cored and deseeded red pepper, cut into wedges, return to the oven and cook for a further 10–20 minutes until the vegetables are soft. Meanwhile, dry-fry the pumpkin seeds in a small nonstick frying pan until toasted, then leave to cool. Place in a food processor or blender with a handful of coriander leaves, ½ chopped green chilli (deseeded, if liked), a squeeze of lime juice and 75 ml (3 fl oz) soured cream and whizz to a sauce. Spoon over the roasted squash and serve.

mexican griddled flatbreads

Makes **8**

Preparation time **20 minutes**, plus rising

Cooking time **20–40 minutes**

450 g (14½ oz) **strong white bread flour**

50 g (2 oz) **polenta**

7 g (¼ oz) sachet **fast-action dried yeast**

1 teaspoon **salt**

350 ml (12 fl oz) **warm water**

75 ml (3 fl oz) **olive oil**, plus extra for brushing

1 teaspoon **cumin seeds**, plus extra to serve

1 **red chilli**, deseeded, if liked, and chopped, plus extra to serve

sea salt flakes, to serve (optional)

Place the flour, polenta, yeast and salt in a bowl and mix together. Add the measurement water, 3 tablespoons of the oil, the cumin seeds and chilli and mix together to form a dough. Knead the dough in an electric mixer for 5 minutes, or by hand on a lightly floured surface for 10 minutes, until the dough is soft and springy. Place in a lightly oiled bowl, cover with clingfilm and leave in a warm place for about 1 hour until the mixture has doubled in size.

Tip the dough out on to a lightly floured surface, then punch it down and knead a couple of times until the air is knocked out. Divide the mixture into 8 equal-sized balls and keep loosely covered with lightly oiled clingfilm. Roll out each ball until 5 mm (¼ inch) thick.

Heat a griddle pan until smoking hot. Brush over the flatbreads with a little oil, then cook, in batches, for 3–5 minutes on each side until lightly charred and cooked through. Tear into large chunks and serve warm, scattered with a little chopped red chilli, some cumin seeds and sea salt flakes, if liked.

For Mexican pizzas, make the dough balls as before and roll out, then place on lightly greased baking sheets. Spread 3 tablespoons tomato pasta sauce over each pizza. Sprinkle over 2 sliced ready-roasted red peppers and 1 drained and sliced pickled jalapeño chilli, then scatter over 150 g (5 oz) grated mozzarella cheese. Bake in a preheated oven, 200°C (400°F), Gas Mark 6, for 10–15 minutes until just cooked through. Scatter with chopped coriander leaves and serve.

deep-fried plantain

Serves **4**
Preparation time **10 minutes**
Cooking time **10 minutes**

3 large ripe **plantains**
vegetable oil, for deep-frying

To serve
chilli flakes
salt flakes

Trim the ends off the plantains. Using a sharp knife, cut a slit along the curve of the fruit all the way through the skins. Peel the skins from the plantains, then cut into 5 mm (¼ inch) slices.

Fill a large saucepan one-third full of oil and heat to 180–190°C (350–375°F), or until a cube of bread browns in 15 seconds. Deep-fry the plantains, in batches, for 2–3 minutes until golden. Remove with a slotted spoon and drain on kitchen paper.

Serve sprinkled with chilli flakes and salt flakes.

For baked plantain, prepare the plantains as above and toss with 3 tablespoons vegetable oil. Spread the slices out on a baking sheet and place in a preheated oven, 180°C (350°F), Gas Mark 4, for 30 minutes, turning once, until soft. Sprinkle with the salt flakes and chilli flakes, if liked.

corn bake with spicy dressing

Serves **4**
Preparation time **15 minutes**
Cooking time **30–40 minutes**

500 g (1 lb) canned or frozen
  sweetcorn, drained or
  defrosted
125 ml (4 fl oz) **single cream**
3 **eggs**, beaten
1 teaspoon **salt**
75 g (3 oz) **butter**

Dressing
125 g (4 oz) **tomatoes**,
  chopped
2 **spring onions**, sliced
1 **red chilli**, deseeded, if liked,
  and chopped
oregano sprig, leaves stripped
  and chopped
salt and **pepper**

Place 400 g (13 oz) of the sweetcorn and the cream in a food processor or blender and whizz until smooth. Add the eggs and salt and blend until well combined. Stir in the remaining sweetcorn.

Melt the butter in a medium-sized baking dish in a preheated oven, 180°C (350°F), Gas Mark 4. Make sure the bottom of the dish is well coated with butter, then pour in the sweetcorn mixture, return to the oven and cook for 30–40 minutes until set.

Meanwhile, make the dressing by stirring together all the ingredients in a bowl. Season well.

Serve spoonfuls of the bake with a little of the tomato dressing spooned over and a dollop of crème fraîche, if liked.

For sweetcorn-stuffed tomatoes, slice off the tops of 4 beef tomatoes using a sharp knife. Scoop out and discard the insides. Heat 1 tablespoon olive oil in a frying pan, add 2 sliced spring onions and 150 g (5 oz) sweetcorn kernels and cook for 3 minutes until soft and lightly browned. Stir in 1 chopped red chilli (deseeded, if liked), 75 g (3 oz) breadcrumbs and 75 g (3 oz) grated Cheddar cheese, then stuff the mixture into the tomatoes. Sprinkle over 1 tablespoon fresh white breadcrumbs and transfer to a baking tray. Drizzle with olive oil and bake in a preheated oven, 200°C (400°F), Gas Mark 6, for 10–15 minutes until the tomatoes are soft.

puddings

chocolate chilli truffles

Makes **25**

Preparation time **15 minutes**,
   plus chilling

Cooking time **5 minutes**

150 ml (¼ pint) **double cream**
25 g (1 oz) **butter**
150 g (5 oz) **plain dark
   chocolate**, chopped
pinch of **chilli powder**, plus
   extra, to serve (optional)
75 g (3 oz) **cocoa powder**

Heat the cream and butter in a small saucepan until the butter melts and the mixture is simmering. Place the chocolate in a heatproof bowl and pour over the hot cream. Add the chilli powder and stir together until the chocolate melts. Chill for at least 4 hours until firm.

Using a melon baller or lightly oiled hands, shape the chocolate mixture into small walnut-sized balls. Spread the cocoa powder on a plate, then roll each chocolate ball in the cocoa until well coated.

Transfer to individual paper cases or arrange on a plate and serve, sprinkled with a little extra chilli powder, if liked. The truffles will keep for up to 3 days in the refrigerator.

For white-chocolate-coated truffles, make the truffle mixture as above. Shape into balls, place on a plate and chill for a further 15 minutes to firm up. Meanwhile, melt 125 g (4 oz) white chocolate, broken into pieces, in a small heatproof bowl set over a saucepan of simmering water, making sure the bottom of the bowl does not touch the water. Remove the melted chocolate from the heat and leave to stand for 2 minutes. Pierce each truffle with a cocktail stick or fork, then dip into the melted chocolate until well coated. Place on a plate lined with nonstick baking paper and dust with extra chilli powder, if liked. Chill until set.

caramelized tequila pineapple

Serves **6**

Preparation time **10 minutes**

Cooking time **10 minutes**

25 g (1 oz) **butter**

1 **pineapple**, skinned, cored and thickly sliced (or shop-bought prepared pineapple slices)

50 g (2 oz) **soft brown sugar**

3 tablespoons **tequila**

juice of ½ **lime**

vanilla ice cream, to serve

Heat the butter in a large frying pan, add the pineapple, in batches if necessary, and cook for 1 minute on each side until golden. Sprinkle over the sugar and cook for a further 2 minutes until it starts to caramelize. Remove the pineapple from the pan.

Pour in the tequila and lime juice, bring to the boil and cook for 1 minute until the mixture starts to thicken. Return the pineapple to the pan and coat in the sauce.

Transfer to serving plates and drizzle over any remaining sauce. Serve with scoops of ice cream.

For griddled pineapple with tequila, lightly brush the prepared pineapple slices with vegetable oil. Cook the pineapple in a griddle or on a medium-hot barbecue for about 5 minutes, turning once, until nicely charred all over. Meanwhile, stir together 6 tablespoons clear honey, 1 tablespoon tequila and a squeeze of lime juice in a bowl. Serve the griddled pineapple drizzled with the sauce.

caramel & banana bread pudding

Serves **6**

Preparation time **15 minutes**, plus soaking

Cooking time **50–60 minutes**

50 g (2 oz) **butter**, softened
8 slices of **brioche bread**
6 tablespoons **dulce de leche**
2 **bananas**
300 ml (½ pint) **milk**
300 ml (½ pint) **double cream**
3 **eggs**
1 teaspoon **ground cinnamon**
25 g (1 oz) **caster sugar**

Butter the brioche on both sides, then spread 4 tablespoons of the dulce de leche over 4 of the slices. Top each with another slice of bread. Cut into rough squares and arrange in a greased baking dish. Slice 1 of the bananas and scatter over the brioche.

Mash the remaining banana in a bowl, add the remaining ingredients and whisk together. Pour over the bread and leave to soak for 30 minutes.

Dot the remaining dulce de leche over the top of the pudding. Bake in a preheated oven, 160°C (325°F), Gas Mark 3, for 50–60 minutes until puffed and just cooked through.

For banana & caramel French toast, mash 2 bananas, then spread over 3 slices of brioche bread. Sandwich the slices together with another 3 slices of brioche. Beat together 3 eggs, 100 ml (3½ fl oz) single cream and ½ teaspoon ground cinnamon in a shallow bowl. Dip both sides of each sandwich into the mixture, leaving each to soak for 1 minute. Heat a small knob of butter in a large nonstick frying pan, add the sandwiches in batches and cook for 2–3 minutes on each side until golden. Serve drizzled with dulce de leche.

iced chocolate mousses

Serves **6**

Preparation time **30 minutes**, plus cooling and freezing

Cooking time **10 minutes**

250 g (8 oz) **plain dark chocolate bar**

15 g (½ oz) **unsalted butter**

2 tablespoons **liquid glucose**

3 tablespoons **fresh orange juice**

3 **eggs**, separated

200 ml (7 fl oz) **double cream**

Make chocolate curls by paring the underside of the block of chocolate with a swivel-bladed vegetable peeler. If the curls are very small, microwave the chocolate in 10-second bursts on full power until the chocolate is soft enough to shape. When you have enough curls to decorate 6 mousses, set aside, then break the remaining chocolate (200 g/7 oz) into pieces.

Melt the chocolate pieces in a heatproof bowl set over a saucepan of gently simmering water, making sure the bottom of the bowl does not touch the water. Stir the butter and glucose into the melted chocolate, then mix in the orange juice. Stir in the egg yolks one at a time until the mixture is smooth. Remove the bowl from the pan and leave to cool.

Whisk the egg whites in a clean bowl until soft peaks form. Whip the cream in a separate bowl until it forms soft swirls. Fold the cream, then the egg whites, into the chocolate mixture.

Pour the mixture into 6 freezer-proof coffee cups or ramekin dishes. Freeze for 4 hours or overnight until firm. Serve decorated with the chocolate curls.

For chilled chocolate & coffee mousses, omit the chocolate curls, glucose and orange juice. Melt 200 g (7 oz) plain dark chocolate as above, then add the butter, 3 tablespoons strong black coffee and the egg yolks. Fold in the whisked egg whites, then pour the mixture into 6 small dishes and chill for 4 hours until set. Whip 125 ml (4 fl oz) double cream until it forms soft swirls, then fold in 2 tablespoons coffee cream liqueur. Spoon on top of the mousses and decorate with sifted cocoa powder.

passion fruit cheesecake

Serves **10**

Preparation time **15 minutes**,
plus cooling and chilling

Cooking time **50 minutes**

600 g (1 ¼ lb) **full-fat cream
cheese**

175 g (6 oz) **caster sugar**

2 tablespoons **plain flour**

1 teaspoon **vanilla extract**

2 **eggs**, plus 1 **egg yolk**

300 ml (½ pint) **soured cream**

3 **passion fruits**

Base

125 g (4 oz) **digestive
biscuits**

50 g (2 oz) **butter**, melted

1 tablespoon **caster sugar**

Make the base. Place the biscuits in a food processor or blender and whizz until small crumbs form. Alternatively, place the biscuits in a plastic food bag, seal and crush with a rolling pin. Mix together the biscuit crumbs, melted butter and sugar. Press the crumbs into the base of a lightly greased 20 cm (8 inch) spring-form cake tin. Bake in a preheated oven, 180°C (350°F), Gas Mark 4, for 10 minutes until crisp.

Meanwhile, beat the cream cheese in a bowl for 1 minute until smooth, then add the sugar, flour, vanilla extract, eggs and egg yolk and half the soured cream and beat together until smooth. Spoon the mixture into the tin, return to the oven and bake for a further 40 minutes until just set. Leave to cool in the tin, then chill overnight.

When ready to serve, stir the remaining cream until smooth. Remove the cheesecake from the tin and place on a serving plate, then spoon over the cream. Halve the passion fruits and spoon the seeds and pulp over the cake.

For passion fruit cheesecake pots, crush 10 digestive biscuits as above until fine crumbs, then divide among 10 glasses. Beat together 200 g (7 oz) cream cheese and 200 g (7 oz) mascarpone cheese in a bowl until smooth. Whisk together 150 ml (¼ pint) double cream and 100 g (3½ oz) caster sugar in a separate bowl until stiff peaks form, then carefully fold in the cream cheese mixture. Divide among the glasses, then top with the passion fruit pulp as above.

coconut rice pudding

Serves **4**

Preparation time **5 minutes**,
   plus cooling

Cooking time **35 minutes**

100 g (3½ oz) **pudding rice**
500 ml (17 fl oz) **milk**
50 g (2 oz) **caster sugar**
grated rind of ½ **orange**
400 ml (13 fl oz) can **coconut
   milk**

Raisin syrup
50 g (2 oz) **dark brown sugar**
1 tablespoon **water**
¼ teaspoon **ground
   cinnamon**
50 g (2 oz) **raisins**
5 tablespoons **double cream**

Place the rice, milk, caster sugar and orange rind in a saucepan and bring just to the boil, then reduce the heat and simmer for 25 minutes, stirring frequently, until the rice is soft, adding more milk if necessary.

Pour in half the coconut milk, bring to the boil and cook for a further 5 minutes until almost all the liquid has evaporated. Stir in the remaining coconut milk, then remove the pan from the heat and leave to cool, stirring occasionally to prevent a skin forming.

Meanwhile, make the raisin syrup. Place the brown sugar and measurement water in a small saucepan and heat until the sugar has dissolved, then cook for a couple of minutes until syrupy. Stir in the cinnamon, raisins and cream.

Spoon the rice pudding into serving bowls and drizzle over the raisin syrup.

For creamy coconut rice brûlée, make the rice pudding as above, adding 25 g (1 oz) raisins to the pudding with the coconut milk. Transfer the cooked rice to 4 heatproof ramekins and chill for 2 hours. When ready to serve, sprinkle 1 tablespoon caster sugar over each pudding and cook under a preheated hot grill or use a chef's blowtorch to caramelize the tops.

watermelon & tequila granita

Serves **6**

Preparation time **20 minutes**,
  plus infusing and freezing

Cooking time **2 minutes**

1 **vanilla pod**
150 g (5 oz) **caster sugar**
150 ml (¼ pint) **water**
2 kg (4 lb) **watermelon**
2 tablespoons **lemon juice**
4 tablespoons **tequila**

Using a small, sharp knife, score the vanilla pod lengthways through to the centre. Put it in a saucepan with the sugar and measurement water. Heat gently until the sugar has dissolved, then remove from the heat and leave to infuse for 20 minutes.

Slice the watermelon into wedges and cut away the skin. Place the flesh in a food processor or blender and whizz until smooth, or rub through a sieve.

Remove the vanilla pod from the syrup, scrape out the seeds with the tip of a knife and add to the syrup, then beat until well mixed. Discard the pod.

Strain the watermelon purée into a freezer-proof container and stir in the vanilla syrup, lemon juice and tequila. Freeze for 3–4 hours until it is turning mushy. Mash with a fork and refreeze for 2–3 hours until it reaches the mushy stage again. Repeat the process once or twice more until the granita is evenly mushy. Freeze until required.

When ready to serve, fork through the granita to break up the ice and pile into 6 tall glasses. Serve with long spoons.

For blackberry & apple granita, heat 300 ml (½ pint) water and 25 g (1 oz) caster sugar in a saucepan until the sugar has dissolved. Add 4 peeled, cored and diced large Gala apples and 150 g (5 oz) blackberries, then cover and simmer for 10 minutes. Cool, then purée and mix with 300 ml (½ pint) extra water. Freeze as above until flakes of ice begin to form.

sugared cinnamon chips

Serves **6**
Preparation time **5 minutes**
Cooking time **10–12 minutes**

50 g (2 oz) **butter**
4 **wheat tortillas**
3 tablespoons **caster sugar**
1 teaspoon **ground cinnamon**

To serve
vanilla ice cream
fresh fruit, such as
   strawberries

Heat the butter in a small saucepan until melted, then brush all over the tortillas. Stir together the sugar and cinnamon in a small bowl, then sprinkle over the tortillas until well coated.

Cut the coated tortillas into equal triangles or strips and place on a baking sheet. Bake in a preheated oven, 200°C (400°F), Gas Mark 6, for 7–10 minutes until crisp.

Serve the tortilla chips with scoops of vanilla ice cream and fresh fruit.

For fruit-filled tortilla cups, cut the tortillas into 12 cm (5 inch) diameter rounds. Wrap in foil and place in a preheated oven, 190°C (375°F), Gas Mark 5, for 2 minutes until pliable. Brush over the butter and sprinkle with cinnamon sugar. Press each tortilla into a large muffin cup or very small ovenproof bowl. Return to the oven and cook for a further 10 minutes until golden and crisp. Remove the tortillas from the muffin cups and leave to cool. Lightly whisk 200 ml (7 fl oz) double cream, 1 tablespoon caster sugar and 1 teaspoon vanilla extract in a bowl. Spoon into the cooled tortilla cups, then top with fresh fruit, such as chopped strawberries and mango slices.

margarita lime pie

Serves **8–10**
Preparation time **20 minutes**,
  plus cooling and chilling
Cooking time **25–30 minutes**

300 g (10 oz) **digestive
  biscuits**
150 g (5 oz) **butter,** melted
400 g (13 oz) can **sweetened
  condensed milk**
4 **egg yolks**
grated rind and juice of
  4 limes
3 tablespoons **tequila**
1 tablespoon **orange liqueur**
2 **egg whites**
300 ml (½ pint) **double cream**
lime slices, to decorate

Place the biscuits in a food processor or blender and whizz until small crumbs form. Alternatively, place the biscuits in a plastic food bag, seal and crush with a rolling pin. Mix together the biscuit crumbs and melted butter, then press into the base and sides of a 22 cm (8½ inch) loose-bottomed tart tin. Bake in a preheated oven, 180°C (350°F), Gas Mark 4, for about 10 minutes until set and lightly browned. Leave to cool.

Mix together the condensed milk, egg yolks, lime rind and juice, tequila and liqueur in a large bowl until well combined. Whisk the egg whites in a separate clean bowl until stiff peaks form, then gently stir into the lime mixture in 3 batches.

Pour the mixture into the prepared base, then return to the oven and bake for 15–20 minutes until the centre is just set. Leave to cool, then chill for at least 2 hours or preferably overnight.

When ready to serve, whip the cream until soft peaks form. Remove the pie from the tin and place on a serving plate. Swirl over the cream, then arrange lime slices on top to decorate.

For margarita milkshake to serve 1, place 100 ml (3½ fl oz) milk, 1 tablespoon tequila, the juice of ½ lime and 1 large scoop of vanilla ice cream in a blender and whizz together. Serve topped with whipped cream and grated lime rind.

almond cookies

Makes **24**

Preparation time **20 minutes**,
  plus cooling and chilling

Cooking time **27–30 minutes**

150 g (5 oz) **blanched
  whole almonds**, plus 24 to
  decorate
125 g (4 oz) **plain flour**
150 g (5 oz) **icing sugar**
¼ teaspoon **ground
  cinnamon**
pinch of **salt**
½ teaspoon **almond extract**
150 g (5 oz) **butter**, softened

Spread the 150 g (5 oz) almonds on a baking sheet and place in a preheated oven, 180°C (350°F), Gas Mark 4, for 7–10 minutes until lightly browned. Leave to cool.

Place the cooled almonds in a food processor or blender and whizz until fine. Pulse in the flour, 100 g (3½ oz) of the icing sugar, the cinnamon and a pinch of salt, then add the almond extract and butter and process until the mixture just comes together to form a dough. Wrap in clingfilm and chill for 30 minutes.

Using your hands, roll the dough into 24 balls. Place on one or two baking sheets lined with nonstick baking paper, spaced apart, then press 1 blanched almond into each one.

Bake in the preheated oven for 20 minutes until lightly browned around the edges. Transfer to a wire rack and leave to cool.

Sift the remaining icing sugar over the cookies and serve with coffee. They will keep for up to 3 days in an airtight container.

For pecan biscuits, make the biscuits as above, replacing the almonds with pecan nuts and adding 25 g (1 oz) finely grated plain dark chocolate with the butter.

mango trifle

Serves **6**
Preparation time **15 minutes**

500 ml (17 fl oz) **fresh
  custard**
2 tablespoons **orange liqueur**
juice of ½ **lime**
200 ml (7 fl oz) **double cream**
2 tablespoons **caster sugar**
2 **mangoes**, peeled, stoned
  and chopped
200 g (7 oz) **soft coconut
  macaroons**, roughly broken
toasted coconut swirls, to
  decorate

Place the custard, liqueur and lime juice in a bowl and mix together. Whisk together the cream and sugar in a separate bowl until soft peaks form.

Tip one-quarter of the chopped mangoes into a mini food processor or blender and whizz until smooth. Mix together with the remaining mango.

Arrange the macaroons in the bottom of 6 serving glasses. Pour over a layer of the custard, then spoon over some of the mango mixture. Repeat the layers, then top each with a generous spoonful of the cream. Serve decorated with toasted coconut swirls.

For mango syllabubs, place half the mangoes in a mini food processor or blender and whizz until smooth. Mix together with the remaining mangoes and spoon into the bottom of 6 serving glasses. Place the grated rind and juice of 2 limes, the orange liqueur, 5 tablespoons caster sugar and 450 ml (¾ pint) double cream in a bowl and whisk until thickened. Spoon over the mango and chill or serve immediately.

mexican rocky road slices

Serves **10**

Preparation time **10 minutes**, plus chilling

Cooking time **5 minutes**

300 g (10 oz) **plain dark chocolate**, broken into pieces

100 g (3½ oz) **milk chocolate**, broken into pieces

100 g (3½ oz) **butter**

3 tablespoons **golden syrup**

75 g (3 oz) **cinnamon** or **almond biscuits**, broken into small pieces

75 g (3 oz) **whole blanched almonds**, toasted

50 g (2 oz) **golden raisins**

1 piece of **candied orange peel**, finely chopped

cocoa powder, for dusting

Melt the dark and milk chocolates, butter and golden syrup in a small heatproof bowl set over a saucepan of simmering water, stirring occasionally and making sure the bottom of the bowl does not touch the water. Stir in the biscuits, almonds, raisins and orange peel.

Line a 10 x 30 cm (4 x 12 inch) terrine dish or loaf tin with clingfilm. Spoon the mixture into the tin and smooth over the surface. Chill for at least 3 hours.

Turn the refrigerator cake out of the tin on to a board, then lightly dust with cocoa powder. Serve cut into slices.

For chilli & orange chocolate slices, make the recipe as above, omitting the biscuits and raisins and stirring in 150 g (5 oz) mixed toasted almonds and hazelnuts and ½ finely chopped red chilli with the candied orange peel.

flan

Serves **6**
Preparation time **10 minutes**,
  plus cooling and chilling
Cooking time **25–30 minutes**

150 g (5 oz) **caster sugar**
4 tablespoons **water**
300 g (10 oz) **sweetened
  condensed milk**
4 **eggs**
300 ml (½ pint) **milk**
1 teaspoon **vanilla extract**

Tip the sugar into a small saucepan, add the measurement water and cook over a low heat until the sugar has dissolved, then increase the heat and cook until the sugar turns dark brown. Pour a little of the liquid into each of 6 individual metal dariole moulds and leave to cool.

Whisk together the condensed milk and eggs in a bowl, then add the milk and vanilla extract and stir together until well combined. Pour the mixture into the dariole moulds and place in a deep baking dish. Pour in boiling water until it comes halfway up the sides of the moulds.

Place in a preheated oven, 160°C (325°F), Gas Mark 3, for 15–20 minutes until just set but still with a slight wobble at the centres. Leave to cool, then chill for at least 4 hours or preferably overnight.

When ready to serve, run a knife around each mould, invert on to a serving plate and then give a gentle tap to remove the flan from the tin. Drizzle over any remaining caramel.

For coffee caramel flan, make the caramel as above and divide among the dariole moulds. Place the milk and 2 teaspoons instant coffee in a saucepan and heat until boiling, stirring until well combined. Stir together the milk, condensed milk and eggs, omitting the vanilla extract and adding 25 g (1 oz) caster sugar. Continue as above.

chocolate orange pudding pots

Serves **6**
Preparation time **15 minutes**,
    plus cooling and chilling
Cooking time **20–25 minutes**

400 ml (14 fl oz) **single cream**
150 ml (¼ pint) **milk**
200 g (7 oz) **plain dark
    chocolate**, chopped
75 g (3 oz) **caster sugar**, plus
    1 tablespoon
1 tablespoon finely grated
    orange rind
3 **eggs**, plus 2 **egg yolks**
100 ml (3½ fl oz) **double
    cream**
strips of **candied orange peel**
    or finely grated **orange rind**,
    to decorate

Place the cream and milk in a saucepan and bring just to the boil. Place the chocolate in a small heatproof bowl and pour over the hot cream. Stir together until the chocolate melts, then leave to cool slightly.

Whisk together the 75 g (3 oz) sugar, the orange rind, eggs and egg yolks in a separate bowl, then gradually whisk in the cooled chocolate mixture.

Place 6 ramekins in a deep baking tin. Divide the mixture among the ramekins, then pour boiling water into the tin until it comes halfway up the sides of the dishes. Bake in a preheated oven, 160°C (325°F), Gas Mark 3, for 15–20 minutes until just set but still with a slight wobble in the centres. Leave to cool, then chill for at least 2 hours or overnight.

When ready to serve, whip together the cream and remaining sugar until soft peaks form. Spoon a little of the cream into each dish and top with strips of candied orange peel or finely grated orange rind.

For boozy chocolate orange brûlée, make the recipe as above, adding 1–2 tablespoons orange liqueur when whisking the sugar, orange rind and juice and eggs. When ready to serve, scatter 2 teaspoons caster sugar over each ramekin. Place under a preheated very hot grill for 1 minute or use a chef's blowtorch to caramelize the sugar.

mexican three-milk cake

Serves **8–10**

Preparation time **15 minutes**, plus cooling

Cooking time **35 minutes**

5 eggs

175 g (6 oz) **caster sugar**

1 teaspoon **vanilla extract**

150 g (5 oz) **plain flour**

2 teaspoons **baking powder**

125 g (4 oz) **butter**, melted

200 ml (7 fl oz) **sweetened condensed milk**

200 ml (7 fl oz) **evaporated milk**

200 ml (7 fl oz) **milk**

To decorate

200 ml (7 fl oz) **double cream**

1 tablespoon **caster sugar**

selection of **fruit**, such as strawberries, blueberries and oranges

Beat together the eggs and sugar in a bowl until pale and thickened. Add the vanilla extract, then gradually stir in the flour and baking powder. Carefully stir in the melted butter until well combined.

Pour the mixture into a lightly greased and base-lined 23 cm (9 inch) cake tin. Bake in a preheated oven, 180°C (350°F), Gas Mark 4, for 30–35 minutes until golden and a skewer inserted into the centre comes out clean.

Whisk together all three milks in a bowl. Prick all over the warm cake with a skewer, then spoon over the milk mixture, letting it sink in. Leave to cool.

When ready to serve, whisk together the cream and 1 tablespoon sugar in a bowl until soft peaks form. Spoon over the cake, then top with the fruit.

For Mexican fruit pots, heat 450 ml (¾ pint) double cream together with 100 ml (3½ fl oz) condensed milk. Let boil for 2 minutes, stirring often. Take off the heat and stir through the juice of 5 limes and the finely grated rind of 1 lime. Pour into 4 serving dishes, then chill in the fridge for at least 3 hours. Decorate with a selection of fruit.

chocolate sorbet

Serves **6**

Preparation time **5 minutes**,
  plus cooling, churning and
  freezing

Cooking time **15 minutes**

200 g (7 oz) **dark muscovado
  sugar**
50 g (2 oz) **cocoa powder**
1 teaspoon **instant espresso
  coffee powder**
1 **cinnamon stick**
600 ml (1 pint) **water**
12 **chocolate coffee
  matchsticks**
2 tablespoons **chocolate
  liqueur**, to serve

Place the sugar, cocoa powder, coffee, cinnamon stick
and measurement water in a large saucepan and slowly
bring to the boil, stirring until the sugar has dissolved.
Boil for 5 minutes, then leave to cool. Remove the
cinnamon stick.

Pour the cooled liquid into a freezer-proof container,
seal and freeze for 2–4 hours until firm. Transfer the
mixture to a food processor or blender and whizz until
smooth, then pour into a 1 kg (2 lb) loaf tin and freeze
for 2 hours, or until frozen solid. Alternatively, place in an
ice-cream maker and churn for 30 minutes until frozen,
then pour into a loaf tin and freeze for 2 hours.

Turn the sorbet out on to a serving plate and arrange
the coffee matchsticks over the top to decorate. Cut
into slices to serve and drizzle 1 teaspoon chocolate
liqueur around each portion.

For chocolate peppermint sorbet, make the sorbet
as above, replacing the coffee and cinnamon stick with
1 teaspoon peppermint extract. To serve, scoop into
balls and place in individual glasses, decorating each
with a mint sprig and serving with 2 or 3 chocolate
peppermint matchsticks.

fresh melon sorbet

Serves **4–6**

Preparation time **15 minutes**, plus freezing

1 **cantaloupe melon,**
  weighing 1 kg (2 lb)
50 g (2 oz) **icing sugar**
juice of **1 lime** or small **lemon**
1 **egg white**

Cut the melon in half and scoop out and discard the seeds. Scoop out the melon flesh with a spoon and discard the shells.

Place the flesh in a food processor or blender with the icing sugar and lime or lemon juice and process to a purée. (Alternatively, rub through a sieve.) Pour into a freezer container, cover and freeze for 2–3 hours. If using an ice-cream maker, purée then pour into the machine, churn and freeze until half-frozen.

Whisk the melon mixture to break up the ice crystals, then whisk the egg white until stiff and whisk it into the half-frozen melon mixture. Return to the freezer until firm. Alternatively, add whisked egg white to the ice-cream machine and churn until very thick.

Transfer the sorbet to the fridge 20 minutes before serving to soften slightly or scoop straight from the ice-cream machine. Scoop the sorbet into glass dishes to serve. To make differently coloured sorbets, make up three batches of sorbet using a cantaloupe melon in one and honeydew and watermelon in the others.

drinks

watermelon cooler

Makes **2**

Preparation time **10 minutes**,
plus freezing

100 g (3½ oz) **watermelon**
100 g (3½ oz) **strawberries**,
hulled
100 ml (3½ fl oz) **still water**
small handful of **mint** or
tarragon leaves, plus extra
to serve (optional)

Skin and deseed the watermelon and chop the flesh into cubes. Hull the strawberries. Freeze the watermelon and strawberries until solid.

Put the frozen watermelon and strawberries in a food processor or blender, add the water and the mint or tarragon and process until smooth.

Pour the mixture into 2 short glasses, decorate with mint or tarragon leaves, if liked, and serve immediately.

For melon & almond smoothie, process 100 g (3½ oz) frozen galia melon flesh with 100 ml (3½ fl oz) almond milk.

mexican marshmallow mocha

Makes **2**
Preparation time **10 minutes**

4 teaspoons **cocoa powder**,
  plus extra to decorate
2 measures **Kahlúa coffee
  liqueur**
7 measures hot **filter coffee**
mini marshmallows
whipped cream

Divide the cocoa powder between 2 hot toddy glasses, add the Kahlúa and coffee and stir until mixed.

Drop in marshmallows and top with whipped cream. Dust with cocoa powder and serve.

For Irish coffee, warm 2 hot toddy glasses and add 1 teaspoon sugar and 1 measure Irish whiskey to each one. Fill the glasses two-thirds full with hot filter coffee and stir until the sugar has dissolved. Float lightly whipped double cream over the top, pouring it over the back of a cold spoon, then serve sprinkled with coffee granules, if liked.

mexican mule

Makes **2**
Preparation time **5 minutes**

2 **limes**, cut into wedges
2 dashes of **sugar syrup**
crushed ice
2 measures **José Cuervo Gold tequila**
2 measures **Kahlúa coffee liqueur**
ginger ale, to top up

Divide the lime wedges between 2 highball glasses and mix together with the sugar syrup using a muddling stick.

Half-fill each glass with crushed ice, add the tequila and Kahlúa, then stir. Top up with ginger ale and serve.

For a Moscow mule, put 6–8 cracked ice cubes in a cocktail shaker, add 4 measures vodka and the freshly squeezed juice of 4 limes and shake well. Pour, without straining, into 2 highball glasses over ice and top up with ginger beer.

tijuana sling

Makes **2**
Preparation time **5 minutes**

3½ measures **tequila**
1½ measures **crème de cassis**
1½ measures **lime juice**
4 dashes of **Peychaud's bitters**
ice cubes
7 measures **ginger ale**

To decorate
lime slices
blueberries

Place the tequila, crème de cassis, lime juice and bitters in a cocktail shaker. Add 8–10 ice cubes and shake vigorously.

Pour into 2 highball glasses without straining and top up with the ginger ale. Decorate with lime slices and blueberries and serve.

For a Border Crossing, replace the tequila with 3½ measures tequila gold, then add 2 measures lime juice, 1 teaspoon honey and several dashes of orange bitters and continue as above.

margarita

Makes **2**
Preparation time **5 minutes**

2 **lime wedges**
rock salt
4 measures **Herrudura Reposado tequila**
2 measures **lime juice**
2 measures **Triple Sec**
ice cubes
lime slices, to decorate

Rub the rims of 2 margarita (coupette) glasses with the lime wedges, then dip them into rock salt.

Pour the tequila, lime juice and Triple Sec into a cocktail shaker and add some ice cubes. Shake, then strain into the salt-rimmed glasses. Decorate each glass with a slice of lime and serve.

For a Grand Margarita, make the recipe as above, replacing the Triple Sec with 2 measures Grand Marnier. This brings a sweet twist to the classic Margarita.

baja sour

Makes **2**
Preparation time **5 minutes**

ice cubes
2½ measures **tequila gold**
4 teaspoons **sugar syrup**
2½ measures **lemon juice**
4 dashes of **orange bitters**
1 **egg white**
2 tablespoons **Amontillado sherry**

To decorate
lemon wedges
orange rind spirals

Place 8–10 ice cubes in a cocktail shaker with the tequila, sugar syrup, lemon juice, bitters and egg white and shake vigorously.

Pour into 2 highball glasses and drizzle over the sherry. Decorate each glass with lemon wedges and an orange rind spiral and serve.

For a Batanga, dip a lime wedge in some salt and rub it around the rim of 2 highball glasses. Fill the glasses with ice, add 2 measures tequila to each and top up with cola.

silk stocking

Makes **2**
Preparation time **5 minutes**

drinking chocolate powder
1½ measures **tequila**
1½ measures **white crème de cacao**
7 measures **single cream**
4 teaspoons **grenadine**
ice cubes

Dampen the rims of 2 chilled martini glasses and dip them into the drinking chocolate powder.

Pour the tequila, crème de cacao, cream and grenadine into a cocktail shaker and add 8–10 ice cubes. Shake vigorously for 10 seconds, then strain into the chilled martini glasses.

For a Sombrero, make the recipe as above, omitting the grenadine. Decorate with grated nutmeg and serve.

mexican bulldog

Makes **2**

Preparation time **5 minutes**

ice cubes

1½ measures **tequila**

1½ measures **Kahlúa coffee liqueur**

2½ measures **single cream**

7 measures **cola**

drinking chocolate powder, to decorate

Place 4–6 ice cubes in 2 highball glasses. Pour in the tequila, Kahlúa and cream, then top up with the cola.

Stir gently, dust with drinking chocolate powder and serve.

For a Brave Bull, fill a tumbler with ice cubes, then add equal measures of tequila and Kahlúa.

tequila slammer

Makes **2**
Preparation time **3 minutes**

2 measures **tequila gold**
2 measures chilled
   Champagne

Pour the tequila into 2 shot glasses. Slowly top up with chilled Champagne.

Cover the top of the glass with the palm of your hand to seal the contents inside and grip it with your fingers. Briskly pick up the glass and slam it down on a surface to make the drink fizz. Quickly gulp it down in one, while it's still fizzing.

For The Raft, combine 2 measures each of vodka and bitter lemon. Pour them into 2 shot glasses, cover with your hand and slam down 3 times. Drink while it's still fizzing.

Rattlesnake

Makes **2**

Preparation time **5 minutes**

ice cubes, plus extra to serve
3 measures **whisky**
2 teaspoons **lemon juice**
2 teaspoons **sugar syrup**
2 **egg whites**
few drops of **Pernod**
lime wedges, to serve

Place 8–10 ice cubes, the whisky, lemon juice, sugar syrup, egg whites and Pernod in a cocktail shaker and shake extremely well.

Strain into 2 tumblers, add some more ice and serve with lime wedges.

For a Kicker, to serve 1, mix 1 measure whisky with 1 measure Midori and serve chilled or with ice.

index

236

acknowledgements

Executive editor: Eleanor Maxfield
Editor: Alex Stetter
Art direction and design: Penny Stock
Photographer: Lis Parsons
Home economist: Emma Lewis
Stylist: Liz Hippisley
Production controller: Sarah Kramer

Picture acknowledgements:
Octopus Publishing Group: Stephen Conroy 75, 105, 125, 211, 217, 219, 221, 223, 225, 227, 229, 231; Will Heap 185, 209; William Lingwood 81, 85; David Munns 113, 119, 139; Sean Myers 95; Lis Parsons 99; Gareth Sambidge 191, 215; William Shaw 131; Ian Wallace 91. Thinkstock: iStock 10.